THE
POCKET BOOK
OF
SPURS

By Martin Cloake

For Cath, Daniel and Tom –
loyal supporters

Published by
Vision Sports Publishing in 2010

Vision Sports Publishing
19-23 High Street
Kingston upon Thames
Surrey
KT1 1LL

www.visionsp.co.uk

WICE ONE CYRIL!

Text © Martin Cloake
Illustrations © Bob Bond Sporting Caricatures

ISBN: 978–1905326-94-5

Series editor: Jim Drewett
Series production: Martin Cloake
Design: Neal Cobourne
Illustrations: Bob Bond
Cover photography: Paul Downes, Objective Image
All pictures: Getty Images

Printed and bound in China by Toppan Printing Co Ltd

A CIP catalogue record for this book is available from the British Library

THIS IS AN UNOFFICIAL PUBLICATION

All statistics in *The Pocket Book of Spurs* are correct up until the
end of the 2009/10 season.

CONTENTS

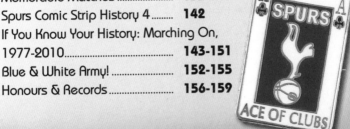

FOREWORD BY
RICKY VILLA

RICARDO
VILLA
TOTTENHAM HOTSPUR

England for me is Tottenham Hotspur. When I was playing in Argentina, Spurs were not a club we heard much about, so as soon as I arrived here with Ossie Ardiles in 1978 I was surprised at how big it was. It was very professional, and it had a great history. We felt very lucky because we decided to come before we knew just what a great club we were joining.

The club did everything to help us concentrate on playing football. And the fans soon let us know what sort of football they wanted. At the training ground they loved to talk football with the players. Every fan wants their club to win all the time, and Spurs fans are no different. I love their passion and the style they demand.

I spent some of the best years of my life playing for this club, so I'm very pleased to introduce and recommend this book to you – a book which contains so much about what makes Spurs such a special club. It's also a great honour for me to feature in these pages. In the section on *Great Goals* is my strike at Wembley in 1981. I can't believe that after so many years people still remember that goal in such detail – although so many people have told me they were there that night I think the crowd must have been about one million, not 90,000! I just feel very lucky that I was in the right place at the right time.

I still look out for Spurs wherever I am and I love coming back to England to see them play. Harry Redknapp's team is an exciting one to watch and I am confident there are some more great stories about to be written in the history of a great club.

...CLUB DIRECTORY...

Club address:

Tottenham Hotspur Football Club

Bill Nicholson Way

748 High Road

Tottenham

London N17 0AP

General club enquiries: 0844 499 5000

Ticket sales: 0844 844 0102(UK)

+44 207 998 1068 (International)

Disabled supporters: 0208 356 5161

Club website: www.tottenhamhotspur.com

One Hotspur Membership: 0844 844 0102,

email: onehotspur@tottenhamhotspur.com

MARTIN PETERS
Tottenham

Spurs retail: 0844 499 5000

Online Megastore:

http://shop.tottenhamhotspur.com/
spurs08/

Stadium tours: 0844 844 0102

Corporate hospitality:

0208 365 5010,

email: corporate.hospitality@tottenhamhotspur.com

Spurs Soccer Schools: 0208 365 5049

Tottenham Hotspur Foundation:

foundation@tottenhamhotspur.co.uk

Tottenham Hotspur Supporters Trust:

www.tottenhamtrust.com

Tottenham Tribute Trust:

www.tottenhamtributetrust.com

TOT. HOTSPUR

GOALKEEPER
PAT JENNINGS

IF YOU KNOW YOUR HISTORY
THE EARLY DAYS
1882-1921

Hotspur Football Club was formed at a meeting of a group of schoolboys beneath a gas lamp on the corner of Park Lane and Tottenham High Road in 1882. Pupils of St John's Middle School had formed the Hotspur Cricket Club two years before and now the boys wanted something to do during the winter months. The name Hotspur was chosen in honour of Sir Henry Percy, a medieval knight whose family were, by the 1880s, major landowners in Tottenham. The boys had learned in school history lessons of the exploits of Sir Henry, nicknamed 'Hotspur' because of his derring do on the battlefield, and so was born one of the most distinctive club names in world football.

Cricket was soon forgotten as a passion for football took hold and the club became established, thanks largely to the efforts of local Reverend John Ripsher who encouraged the boys to put the club on a formal footing. In 1883 Hotspur FC, playing on a pitch at the Park Lane end of Tottenham Marshes, began their first organised season with a 9-0 victory over Brownlow Rovers. At around this time the club became Tottenham Hotspur to avoid confusion with another club, London Hotspur.

In those early years only friendlies and cup football matches were played, but Spurs attracted large crowds. The numbers, and instances of rowdy behaviour, meant that playing on public land was becoming impractical, so in 1888 the club moved to a private ground off Northumberland Park. Crowds continued to grow,

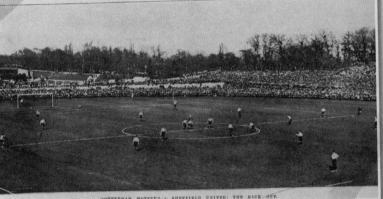

THE ILLUSTRATED LONDON NEWS, APRIL 27, 1901.— 619

THE FOOTBALL ASSOCIATION CUP FINAL TIE AT THE CRYSTAL PALACE, APRIL 20.

PHOTOGRAPHED BY RUSSELL.

TOTTENHAM HOTSPUR v. SHEFFIELD UNITED: THE KICK-OFF.

with support for the club boosted by a widely-ridiculed fine and ground closure imposed on the club in 1893 by the London FA over a supposed incident of "professionalism".

Kick off in the 1901 FA Cup final, dubbed "the greatest football attraction of all time" by the press

The club's growing reputation attracted a better standard of player, allowing them to beat some of the leading sides in the south. But it soon became clear that to progress the club would have to go professional, a decision taken in 1895. The following year the club's application to join the Football League Second Division was turned down. The Southern League, however, accepted Spurs' application and, on the basis of their strong standing in the south, placed them straight into the First Division.

In 1898 Tottenham Hotspur became a limited company, a move intended to secure the financial future of a club now able to attract crowds of 15,000. By now, Northumberland Park was bursting at the seams and in 1899 Spurs moved to a new ground

just off Tottenham High Road – a site which would become the modern White Hart Lane. The club now played in white shirts and blue shorts in honour of the "Invincibles" of Preston North End, who won the Football League and FA Cup Double that season.

Spurs captain Danny Steel tosses up with his Sunderland counterpart before a match in 1912

It was an inspirational choice, as Spurs won the Southern League that season, establishing the club's reputation as 'the flower of the south'.

The following season Spurs became the first, and are still the only, non-League team to win the FA Cup, beating Sheffield United 3-1 in a replay at Burnden Park after an enormous crowd of 114,000 flocked to the first game at Crystal Palace. The result signalled the arrival of southern clubs at football's top table and the beginning of football's modern era. Spurs were led into the final by player-manager-secretary John Cameron, one of the most influential figures in the club's establishment and also in early football. In 1898, Cameron also became secretary of the Association Footballers' Union, the forerunner of the Professional Footballers' Association.

Although the following seasons brought no trophies, Spurs continued to play an entertaining style of football, attracting large crowds and players of the calibre of Vivian Woodward, at the time the country's best centre forward. In 1908 they were admitted to the Football League Second Division and in that first season gained promotion to the top flight. For the next four campaigns Spurs struggled to maintain their place in the First Division and when the League was suspended in 1914 as war swept the globe, Spurs were bottom of the table.

What happened when the game restarted in 1919 laid the seeds of a fierce rivalry that continues to this day. The League intended to expand the top flight

The 1921 Cup winners
show off the trophy

by two places and precedent suggested Spurs would
stay up to be joined by the two sides that finished
top of the Second Division. Instead, Tottenham were
relegated and their place taken by Arsenal, who
had finished sixth in Division Two. The fact that
Arsenal had moved from south London to a ground
close to Tottenham's made them commercial as
well as football rivals and now they had been
handed the ascendancy.

A furious Spurs proceeded to storm back into
the top flight, winning the Second Division title
with a record 70 points. In the following season
they finished sixth in the League and reached the
FA Cup final for the second time thanks largely to
some inspirational performances from inside forward

Jimmy Seed, whose hat-trick in the second round against Bradford City included two goals in 30 seconds.

The final against Wolves was played on a rain-sodden day at Stamford Bridge. Despite the weather, the crowd of 72,000 began arriving early in the morning and the gates were opened at 10.30am. The pitch was a quagmire and both sides struggled, but in the 65th minute Jimmy Dimmock hit a shot from 25 yards out that skimmed the surface on its way into the far corner of the net. The goal secured Tottenham's second FA Cup, but few images of the victory exist because the weather meant most photographers stayed away.

The trophy was carried back to Tottenham via Hyde Park, Camden Town and Seven Sisters in an open charabanc, adorned with the ribbons that had adorned the same trophy after the 1901 victory. At the celebration dinner in Holborn that night, all ten surviving members of that famous victory attended to join the toasts to the club's new heroes.

The victorious Spurs team leave Stamford Bridge with the FA Cup in 1921. The open-topped charabanc carried the players through cheering crowds back to Tottenham

BADGE OF
HONOUR

The boys who formed Hotspur FC initially adopted a gothic H on a red shield that stood out from the navy jerseys, and a stylised white cross was worn on the subsequent blue-and-white-halved shirts. But the club didn't really have a proper shirt badge until 1921, when the cockerel emblem first appeared on the kit.

Captain Arthur Rowe sports the 1950s incarnation of the cockerel

This first badge was a simple blue representation of a cockerel inside a curved navy shield. This remained unchanged for 45 years, a period during which the club experienced its greatest successes – a fact which helps explain the continuing appeal of the simple cockerel image to all associated with Spurs.

The cockerel had become associated with the club because of the founding boys' inspiration, Harry Hotspur. The riding spurs he was said to wear into battle were similar to the spurs worn by fighting cockerels popular in gambling dens in Victorian times. A cockerel began to feature on the club's printed material from 1910,

the same year the copper cockerel was placed on the West Stand.

Left: A stripped down cockerel adorned the shirts of the Double winners

The design of the cockerel remained largely unchanged, save for some details of tail feathers and plumage and an impressive weight loss, until 1965, when a more stylised cockerel standing on a panelled ball with no shield was introduced. It was a simple image that became iconic in an age of classic iconic designs. Stitched in to the shirt in navy on the white home top and in white on the navy away, its very simplicity as the only detail on an uncluttered canvas gave it real presence.

For a short period, the full crest appeared on the team's strip

In 1956, club publicity began to feature a crest, with the cockerel on ball joined by symbols of the local area – a turreted tower, representing Bruce Castle, and seven elm trees from which the Seven Sisters area derived its name. Two lions rampant, which would appear in various guises on shirts and crests over the coming years, also featured, a symbol taken from

the coat of arms of the Percy family, from where Henry 'Hotspur' Percy came. Percy was the son of the Earl of Northumberland, and the local area derives its name from the family's ownership of the land.

In 1980, the cockerel was moved from the left breast to the centre of the shirt, just below the point of the v-neck, where it stayed for two highly successful seasons. In 1982 a curved scroll carrying the words Tottenham Hotspur appeared below the cockerel, now standing on a new ball design, and the dates 1882 and 1982 flanked the symbol to mark the club's centenary. In 1983 the badge on the shirt featured the intertwined letters THFC on the ball, which was flanked by two red lions. The club motto 'Audere Est Facere' (To Dare is To Do) appeared on a yellow scroll below.

Elements of the club crest were introduced so the club could copyright the badge

In 1993 a shield, composed of straight lines, again enclosed the cockerel, lions and scroll, and in 1995 a slightly more aesthetically pleasing shield carrying a stylised cockerel was tried. Both were rather clunky cloth badges stitched on to the shirt, rather than woven in.

By 1997 the full club crest, complete with turrets,

lions and trees on a navy background, appeared on the shirts. This was stripped down to the cockerel, red lions and yellow scroll for the 1999/00 season, a cleaner design with no shield which was woven into the shirts and which remained until the 2006/07 season, when a radical redesign was introduced as part of a new corporate branding exercise.

The current badge has gone down well with fans

The new design represents a modern take on a traditional classic. A simple cockerel is once again the focal point, redrawn "to appear sleek and proud... focussed and alert" according to club publicity. The ball upon which it stands is a unique design based on the copper symbol cast by former player William James Scott and mounted on the old West Stand in 1910. This simple, striking image sits on the left breast of the shirt, stitched in to the fabric. The club crest was also replaced with the same image and the addition of the capitalised words Tottenham Hotspur, set in a gentle curve on two decks below the ball.

Despite the loss of the club motto, fans generally seem to agree with the club statement that the design "reflects our traditions as well as our reputation for style".

THE 1961 DOUBLE

"I can hardly believe what Spurs did that year. Forget Liverpool, forget Manchester United, forget the Brazilians. Compared to Spurs in 1960/61, the others were just donkeys."

Those lines – spoken in the closing sequence of Julie Welch's 1984 film *Those Glory Glory Days* – serve as reminder of how significant the Spurs Double of 1961 was. It had been 64 years since any club had achieved the feat, the last being Preston North End in 1887, although the famous north-western club only played 27 games compared with the 49 played by Bill Nicholson's Spurs. Fittingly enough, in 1898 the Spurs kit of white shirts and blue shorts had been adopted in honour of Preston's achievement.

The season that was to end with the first Double of the modern era began under a cloud, the Spurs first team having been held 4-4 in the traditional public trial match by the reserves. Manager Bill Nicholson said it was the worst performance he'd ever seen. The campaign proper began with a competent 2-0 home win over Everton. The following Monday brought Spurs to Blackpool, where they secured a 3-1 victory that prompted the *Daily Mirror* to dub them 'Super Spurs' for the first time.

On 3rd September Manchester United visited, and were trounced 4-1 in a dazzling performance that confirmed Spurs's title credentials. Seven days later TV cameras broadcast the first ever live game, between Blackpool and Bolton. They should have been at Highbury, where a thrilling exhibition saw Arsenal beaten 3-2 by a superb Spurs. Seven wins on the trot and Spurs had equalled the record set by Preston's 'Invincibles' in 1887.

Beating Leicester 2-1 at Filbert Street saw Spurs equal Hull City's League record of nine wins from the start of the season. In the next game Aston Villa were hammered 6-2. Hull sent a telegram conceding the record. Next came Wolves at Molineux. In a performance described as "soccer magic" by Tom Finney in the *News of the World*, Spurs won 4-0 to rack up a record 11 straight wins.

Then Manchester City came to Spurs and broke the run. A crowd of 60,000 saw Tottenham held 1-1, despite firing in 39 shots to City's nine. Spurs bounced back by beating Nottingham Forest 4-0 in a performance that saw every player score 10 in *The*

Nicholson's Super Spurs parade the FA Cup at Wembley, their status as legends secured

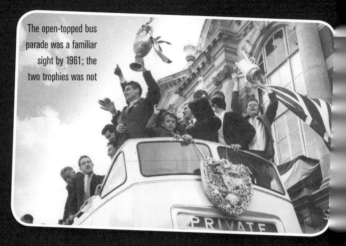

The open-topped bus parade was a familiar sight by 1961; the two trophies was not

People's match report – the first time this had ever happened. Twelve goals in the next three games took the unbeaten run to 16, but the fluent football showed signs of seizing up. Then on 12th November Spurs went to Sheffield Wednesday, a team seven points adrift in second place but unbeaten at home and something of a bogey team. Wednesday beat Spurs 2-1, ending the run and prompting the question "Will Spurs crack?"

After the game, the Spurs players expressed relief that the pressure of maintaining the unbeaten run was over and, in their next game, beat Birmingham City 6-0. They only dropped one more point, to Burnley, until the turn of the year, at which point the bookies stopped taking bets on Spurs winning the title.

In the New Year, Spurs could concentrate on the FA Cup, beating Charlton and Crewe, before knocking out Aston Villa at their bogey ground of Villa Park. Spurs lost a further two League games by the end of February, and in early March Sunderland took them to a cup replay before falling to a five-goal blitz. Spurs won only one of the four League games in March, but secured a place at Wembley by beating Burnley 3-0 at Villa Park. Now they could focus on lifting the League title, and a four-game winning run meant Spurs had to beat Sheffield Wednesday at home on Wednesday 17th April to do so.

The crowds queued from early morning. By kick-off that evening 62,000 were inside. It was a tense game and Spurs went behind in the 19th minute. Just before half-time 50 seconds of majestic football saw Spurs score twice to take the lead, with stunning goals from Bobby Smith and Les Allen.

In *The Express*, Clive Toye wrote of "moments filled with the magic impulse that makes Spurs the great team, the great goal machine, the great champions." The crowd poured onto the pitch and chanted for Danny Blanchflower. Nicholson said he wanted another three points to set the all-time record.

Spurs only managed two points from their last three games, and the Cup Final performance against Leicester City was not one of their best. But as Footballer of the Year Blanchflower collected the Cup, few doubted they were worthy winners of the Double. They had won the first 11 games, still a top-flight record. They had won 31 times in the League, 16 times away from home. Their points total of 66 equalled the record set by Herbert Chapman's Arsenal, the 115 goals they scored was a club record, and they reached 50 points in 29 games, faster than any club had done before.

The significance of the Double may have lessened after 50 years, but the impact of this Double never will. It was the first, it was the most glorious and it will never be matched.

61: The Spurs Double, the official illustrated history marking the 50th anniversary of the Double, was published in August 2010.

SPURS COMIC STRIP HISTORY

1

WHEN SPURS WON THE FA CUP IN 1901, THEY WERE THE FIRST NON-LEAGUE TEAM TO DO SO...

BEFORE THE PRESENTATION, A DIRECTOR'S WIFE TIED SOME RIBBONS TO THE CUP.

SKIPPER JACK JONES LIFTED THE TROPHY. WHEN SPURS NEXT WON THE CUP, IN 1921, THE SAME RIBBONS WERE TIED ON TO IT....

THE LANE

Tottenham Hotspur began playing on the site of the current stadium in 1899, moving from their previous ground in nearby Northumberland Park because greater capacity was needed. The plot of land situated next to the White Hart pub was leased from brewers Charrington on condition that attendances of 1,000 for first team games were guaranteed.

The site was next to the club's established offices at 748 High Road. The ground had a capacity of 30,000, with stands brought over from Northumberland Park providing cover for 2,500 along the west side of the pitch. The stadium was never formally named, simply taking the name of the road which ran close to it, White Hart Lane.

As a result of becoming Southern League champions at the end of their first season at the

Above: One of the earliest photographs of Spurs in action at The Lane, against Blackburn in 1911

ground, the club were able to purchase the freehold for £8,900 and to buy land and houses to the north of it. In 1909, to celebrate reaching Division One, a new West Stand designed by Archibald Leitch was opened. It had 5,300 seats and room for 6,000 standing under a covered paddock at the front. The front of the stand featured a large, mock-Tudor gable with the club's name in ornate lettering and flagpoles adorned each corner of the pitched roof. The directors' and press boxes were situated on the halfway line, the dressing rooms below the stand.

The famous cockerel and ball was added to the

An ambulance worker hands water to the packed crowd at a game in 1913

gable in 1910 and capacity on the east side doubled as the stand roof was removed. The end terraces were also expanded to give a capacity of 40,000. In 1920 the north, Paxton Road, end was covered and in 1923 an almost identical stand was erected at the south, Park Lane, end. The ground now had covered accommodation for 30,000 spectators.

Three of the four stands had been designed by

Leitch and in 1934 he was commissioned to upgrade the East Stand. He did so, presenting the club with the largest and, some said, the finest stand in the country when it opened in 1936. It cost the then extravagant sum of £60,000 and was made up of three tiers. The top contained 5,100 seats, the bottom terrace held 8,000 standing. The middle terrace stretched the length of the pitch, held 11,000 and

Playing up for the cameras in front of the old West Stand in 1961

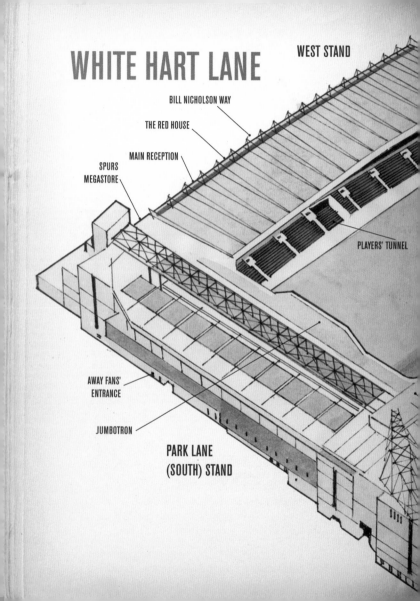

WHITE HART LANE

WEST STAND

BILL NICHOLSON WAY

THE RED HOUSE

MAIN RECEPTION

SPURS
MEGASTORE

PLAYERS' TUNNEL

AWAY FANS'
ENTRANCE

JUMBOTRON

PARK LANE
(SOUTH) STAND

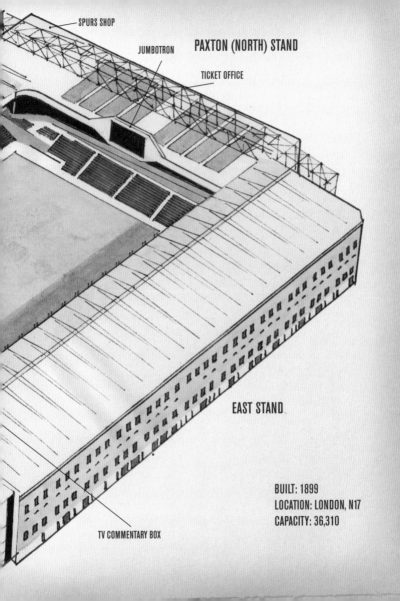

SPURS SHOP

JUMBOTRON

PAXTON (NORTH) STAND

TICKET OFFICE

EAST STAND

TV COMMENTARY BOX

BUILT: 1899
LOCATION: LONDON, N17
CAPACITY: 36,310

provided the finest terraced view in the country, eventually becoming the famous Shelf that hosted the heart of the home support. High in the roof was a large press box. The capacity was now 80,000, with 60,000 covered places.

There were no more major changes until 1952, when the pitch was relaid and the country's most advanced drainage system installed under the new turf. In 1953 floodlights were added, an upgrade in 1957 necessitating the re-siting of the cockerel and ball to the East Stand. In 1961 four floodlight pylons, one in each corner, replaced the previous lighting system. In 1962 a further 3,000 seats were added to the back of the Park Lane stand. The same job was done in the Paxton the next year and this stand was joined to the West, taking capacity down to 60,000. In 1972 new floodlights were installed and the next year a seated section was added to join the corner of the Park Lane and West Stand.

In 1980 Leitch's West Stand was demolished, the first step in a complete redevelopment of the whole ground. The new stand, with only 6,500 seats but 72 executive boxes and new office and corporate facilities, opened in 1982, but the cost had spiralled to £4.2 million and led to the financial difficulties that eventually saw the club taken over by a new board.

In 1988 the East Stand was redeveloped, a move which saw The Shelf replaced with 36 executive boxes. The roof was also remodelled to match that on the West Stand, the press gantry demolished and the

ground's floodlight pylons removed to be replaced
with spotlights mounted on the front of the East
and West stands.

But the stand opened late, leading to an FA fine
after a game was postponed, pillars supporting the
cantilever roof obstructed the view, the compromise
'Ledge' terrace along the front of the boxes was
unpopular, and the £9m cost was high.

The lower terraces of the East and the Park

Bill Brown saves
against Wolves in
1961 in a picture which
shows the famous Shelf
terrace in its pomp

Lane stands were seated in 1992, with the Paxton becoming all-seater a year later. In 1994 seats were installed on the 'Ledge' and the Park Lane demolished. It was replaced a year later with a new structure, complete with Jumbotron TV screen.

The club planned to link all four stands in a wraparound arena and refurbishment work on the Paxton was completed in 1998, with a second Jumbotron screen added and the roof now joined

all around the ground.

The ground now had a capacity of 36,310 and, despite the continental leanings of the wraparound design, the compact set-up still means that the atmosphere traditionally associated with a full-blooded English matchday can be whipped up. In 2007, the *Bolton Evening News* remarked, "It's not the biggest ground in the Premiership, but it's by far the best stage."

In 2008, long-trailed moves to develop a new stadium with a capacity of 56,000 were announced, with extensive consultation resulting in the release of a series of amended proposals in May 2010.

The plan is to construct a modern bowl-shaped stadium just to the north of the current ground. Outside will be a new public space, a supermarket, housing and a hotel built alongside a clutch of historic buildings including The Red House, in which the club's founding members met and where Bill Nicholson and Eddie Baily once sat and made their plans. This mix of tradition and modernity will give the ground a unique feel.

The world famous home of the Spurs as it is today

GREAT GOALS

TERRY DYSON
1963 EUROPEAN CUP-WINNERS' CUP FINAL v ATLETICO MADRID

Diminutive winger Terry Dyson played a big part when Tottenham Hotspur became the first British side to win a European trophy.

Dyson had the game of his life on that famous evening in Rotterdam against highly-fancied Atletico Madrid, the holders. Spurs trounced the Spaniards 5-1, with Dyson setting up two, making the tackle that turned the game, and scoring two.

His second, the Lilywhites' fifth, was a fitting effort with which to cap a triumphant display. Picking up the ball as he drifted in from the left, Dyson exchanged passes with Tony Marchi and pushed on, keeping the ball under control as he picked up pace. Before him, Atletico's once-feared defence backed off en masse. Checking left just outside the penalty box at the end of a 25-yard run, Dyson looked up and, barely breaking his stride, unleashed a shot high into the the top left hand corner of the net, leaving Atletico's keeper a crumpled heap at the foot of his post.

"No one came towards me," Dyson recalled. "I kept going towards goal and when I looked up I could not even see the keeper so I just shot and in it went." As *The Daily Telegraph* reported, "This was Terry Dyson's game."

JIMMY GREAVES
1965 DIVISION ONE v MAN UTD

A classic, flowing Tottenham goal against a defending champions' line-up featuring Best, Charlton, Stiles, Crerand and Law, topped off by England's greatest goalscorer.

Maurice Norman collected the ball deep inside his own half. He checked and laid it off to Alan Mullery. Mullery stepped towards Norman and passed back first time. Norman stepped forward and rolled it back to Mullery, who knocked it back as he was closed down. The pair were goading United's midfielders. As their opponents took the bait, the Spurs pair stepped up a gear, Norman passing forward to Eddie Clayton between two lunging red shirts. Under pressure, Clayton passed to Dave Mackay, who looked up and drove forward to the halfway line. His pass forward to Jimmy Greaves took out another two opponents. Greaves, back to goal and under pressure, controlled tightly and turned in the face of an oncoming tackle, at the same time leaving his original marker trailing. He gathered speed, running diagonally into United's box as five red shirts converged on him. Alan Gilzean's run across Greaves's path sowed further confusion, Greaves rode a tackle and wriggled into the box as keeper Dunne came out to him. Greaves swerved him, ran on and rolled the ball nonchalantly into the net.

"Oohhh, beautiful football, fabulous goal," cried commentator Kenneth Wolstenholme.

MULLERY

NORMAN

CLAYTON

MACKAY

GREAVES

GREAVES

MARTIN CHIVERS
1972 UEFA CUP FINAL, FIRST LEG, v WOLVES

In his classic book *The Glory Game*, Hunter Davies has this to say about the first leg of this domestic tussle for Euro-glory.

"Both sides, knowing each other too well, seemed to be holding back, stuck in their own lethargy, waiting for something to happen. The happening was Chivers."

The big man used to infuriate Bill Nicholson and his assistant Eddie Baily by doing what he did that night; slumbering through the proceedings until suddenly arising to shake the foundations of the opposition. On this occasion, he did it not once, but twice. On 57 minutes he headed home to put Spurs ahead. On 87 he put his side in the driving seat with a superb effort.

Wide on the touchline, he jumped and flicked the ball off the side of his foot. Wolves's John McAlle snaffled the ball, but was immediately dispossessed by a bustling Alan Mullery, who laid the ball short to Chivers on the touchline. Chiv cut inside as Mullery went wide and Gilzean moved square. Driving on at full stretch, Chivers – without appearing to aim or break stride – unleashed a scorching drive that gave Phil Parkes no chance.

"On his own," says Davies, "Chivers had won the match. Apart from the two goals he hadn't done much."

CHIVERS

CHIVERS

MULLERY

RICKY VILLA
1981 FA CUP FINAL REPLAY, v MAN CITY

With the replay finely poised at 2-2 on 77 minutes, Graham Roberts broke up a City attack on the edge of the Spurs box and passed to Tony Galvin on the wing.

Galvin burst forward but, blocked by Ray Ranson and Tommy Caton inside the City half, checked and rolled the ball to Villa.

Villa veered towards the penalty area, swerved left, then right to cut through two of the seven defenders buzzing around him. To his right Steve Archibald waved his arms and screamed for the ball in the space left as City's defenders were drawn to the Argentinian. Behind him Garth Crooks mimed jerky kicks with his right foot. Villa looked as if he would stumble and fall, but instead stretched to poke the ball under the body of the advancing Joe Corrigan. Villa hit the ground as the ball crossed the line, hauled himself up and raced away at speed to his right, a smile of sheer delight lighting up the stadium before his team-mates engulfed him.

It was voted the greatest goal scored at the old Wembley. Ricky says, "When I put my head up, the goal was really close, and I lost control before I should, but it finished in the net. My dream was to score a great goal in a great place."

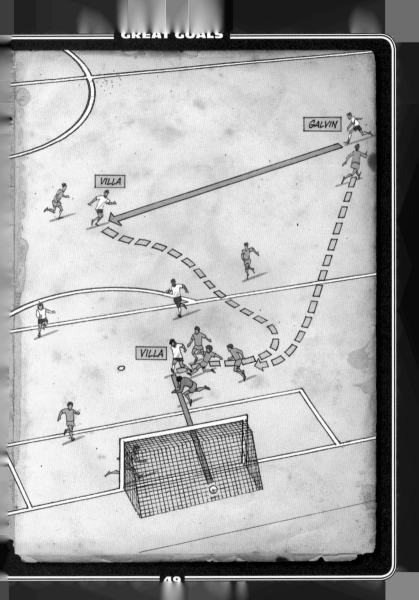

GALVIN

VILLA

VILLA

GLENN HODDLE
1986 DIVISION ONE
v OXFORD UTD

You could write a whole book about Hoddle's goals. This one illustrates not just his unmatched skill, but his relationship with the fans who still worship him.

Tottenham's penultimate home game of the season was against Oxford United. Everyone knew Hoddle would be leaving the club in the summer. And this was his farewell goal. Deep inside his own half, he latched onto a headed clearance from the edge of the Spurs box. Running down the middle of the pitch, he reached the halfway line to be confronted by three defenders playing a high line. With a shimmy and an explosive burst of speed he left them standing.

That task accomplished, he seemed to slow as he loped into the penalty area. With a slick feint he left the keeper on his backside and strode on, oozing complete control as he rolled the ball left into the net. He continued his jog towards the terraces, stopped and raised his arms high for several seconds, blew a double-handed kiss as if to say, "That's yours", and turned back for the restart.

It was the last time he would score in a Spurs shirt, a fitting farewell from a player never since matched.

HODDLE

HODDLE

PAUL GASCOIGNE
1991 FA CUP SEMI-FINAL v ARSENAL

A Spurs team struggling for form, battered by internal strife and on the verge of bankruptcy faced a formidable Arsenal side chasing a League and Cup double in the first FA Cup semi-final to be staged at Wembley.

Gascoigne's goal is not only a classic in its own right, but one of the most important in Spurs's history. Defeat in this game would not only have been a blow to local pride, but possibly dumped debt-ridden Spurs permanently out of the upper orders of English football.

With four minutes gone Gazza, who had been the inspiration behind the cup run, grabbed the ball as Spurs won a free kick some 30 yards from goal. To his right, Paul Stewart moved towards the box, while Gary Lineker advanced from the left. There were three men in the wall. David Seaman, England's goalkeeper, was between the sticks. A direct attempt looked impossible.

But not to Gazza. He thumped a soaring, curving free kick around the wall and into the net. Seaman could only grasp at air as, diving to his left, the ball flashed past him to give Spurs the lead. Commentator Barry Davies described it as "*Schoolboys' Own* stuff". Gascoigne's verdict after the game? "I'm away to get me suit measured."

GASCOIGNE

DANNY ROSE
2010 PREMIER LEAGUE
v ARSENAL

Any goal against Arsenal is special. But sometimes a goal is even more special because of the ramifications it has.

To understand why this goal will go down as one of the greats, it's necessary to understand the background to the game it was scored in.

The season was reaching its climax. Arsenal had clawed their way back into the title race and needed a win to stay in the hunt. Spurs, pushing for the top four, faced the top three sides in consecutive games over the next seven days. An FA Cup semi-final defeat just three days before had raised questions about the team.

Ten minutes into the game, Gareth Bale sent a corner arcing into the box from the line in front of the away section. Manuel Almunia rose to punch far up the pitch. As the ball fell the figure of 19-year-old debutant Danny Rose was seen running towards it. He shaped and caught the ball on the volley with his left foot. It would, said Henry Winter in *The Telegraph*, "have triggered speed cameras on the M11 as it raced 30 yards past the hapless Almunia."

After a nanosecond of stunned silence, the stadium exploded. It was the sweetest of volleys but, more importantly, it gave Spurs belief. They went on to win the derby, the first in the league for 11 years, then to outclass Chelsea and finally to secure fourth on Manchester City's home turf. And it all started with Danny Rose's wonder goal.

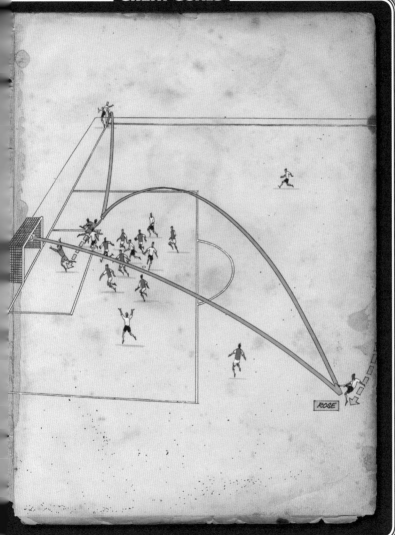

ROSE

THE NORTH LONDON DERBY

Many passions provide fuel for football's great derby rivalries. The Glasgow derby is rooted in the historic divide between Catholic and Protestant; the Barcelona v Real Madrid 'Classico' draws deeply on political and national identity. For some time, the Milan derby reflected Italy's right-left political divide, while the fierce rivalry between River Plate and Boca Juniors in Argentina draws on the class divide between the club's respective supporter bases.

The North London derby is not rooted in any such divisions. No single community follows either one side or the other, no one district is exclusively blue and white or red and white. Instead, the two north London giants have irritated each other intensely for nearly 100 years.

Spurs fans will be quick to point out that the true north London derby is in fact Tottenham v Leyton Orient, as these were the two original league teams to be established north of the river. But in 1913, despite protests from Spurs, Orient and local residents, Arsenal were uprooted from their home in

THE NORTH LONDON DERBY

Woolwich, south east London, and installed at Highbury just down the Seven Sisters Road after Gunners chairman Henry Norris saw the expanding northern suburbs and transport links as a means to build support.

Relations between the two clubs worsened in 1919 when football resumed after the First World War. When the league had been suspended, Spurs had been bottom of Division One while Arsenal had been lying sixth in Division Two. After the war was over the league wanted to expand the top division from 20 to 22 teams, and precedent suggested the bottom two sides should remain in the top flight, to be joined by the second tier's top two. Instead, Arsenal were controversially awarded Tottenham's place!

Norris, who would be banned from football for life in 1929 for flouting FA rules, had been lobbying hard before the shock decision. On the day it was made, the parrot which had lived at White Hart Lane since being awarded to the team after a tour of Argentina keeled over and died – which is where the great football cliché 'sick as a parrot' is said to have originated. Arsenal have remained in the top division ever

Len Duquemin squeezes off a shot in the 1953 derby at Highbury

Ossie Ardiles and Paul Davis
tussle during the 1987
League Cup semi-final

since, the only team
not to achieve top-flight
status on merit.

Between the time
of the Woolwich club's
arrival in north London
and the outbreak of
the Second World War, relations between the respective
boards were understandably frosty therefore although, as was
common in many cities, many fans would go to watch both
clubs on alternate Saturdays.

The 1950s and 60s saw Tottenham cement their reputation
as entertainers while Arsenal languished. Even when the
Gunners matched Spurs' feat of doing the Double in 1971,
Tottenham fans still pointed out the football was functional.

By now relations off the field had taken a turn for the worse,
with violent incidents accompanying many derby matches. But
despite the rituals of hooliganism, fans of both sides still mixed
away from the match and the rivalry was as likely to be marked
by banter as by bashing up.

Through the 70s and 80s Tottenham fans saw 'Boring,
Boring Arsenal' as the anti-football side. But since the Premier
League began, Arsenal have shaken the dull image and, say
their fans, moved ahead to such an extent that the derby no
longer matters to them.

In truth, this is just another in the long line of put-downs

ses. The derby still matters to any north
purs tend to win when it matters most. The
i-final at Wembley was possibly the biggest
Gazza-inspired Spurs securing their future
ng much-fancied Arsenal at Wembley.
derbies with Harry Redknapp at the helm
nal. In his first game in charge, Redknapp
put Spurs ahead with a 40-yard volley, only
to 4-2 down with a minute remaining. But
atched the draw amid wild scenes.
senal came to White Hart Lane for the first
tive games against the top three teams
which would define the season. This time,
dible early volley from young Danny Rose
y to a deserved victory – and one which
s slim title chances.
ondon rivalry does not draw on the deep
her derbies, nearly a century of living
ing for

SPURS COMIC STRIP HISTORY

2

RETURNING FROM A TOUR OF SOUTH AMERICA IN 1908, THE SPURS PLAYERS WERE INVITED TO A SHIP'S FANCY DRESS PARTY. TWO OF THE PLAYERS BORROWED THE SHIP'S PARROT TO ROUND OFF THEIR ROBINSON CRUSOE AND MAN FRIDAY OUTFITS. THEY WON THE COMPETITION AND WERE GIVEN THE PARROT TO KEEP!

THE PARROT LIVED HAPPILY AT WHITE HART LANE FOR YEARS...

PRETTY POLLY! COME ON YOU SPURS!

UNTIL THE DAY ARSENAL WERE AWARDED TOTTENHAM'S PLACE IN DIVISION ONE, IN 1919, WHEN IT FELL FROM ITS PERCH AND SNUFFED IT...

SPURS LOSE DIVISION ONE PLACE TO NEIGHBOURS

IF YOU KNOW YOUR HISTORY
GLORY DAYS
1922-63

The Spurs team managed by Peter McWilliam, having won promotion and the FA Cup in successive seasons, now had its sights set on the League title. But they struggled at the start of the 1921/22 season, before a post-Christmas run of form took them to a second-place finish behind Liverpool – the highest position a London team had ever secured. In the FA Cup, Spurs met Preston in the semi-final, but lost 2-1.

That match was the end of an era. McWilliam's great team broke up and the club's directors refused to fund replacements, preferring instead to rely on bargains and the development of local players. In 1926 Middlesbrough offered to double his wages to £1,700 a year. He told the Spurs directors he wanted to stay, but asked for a small increase to £1,000 a year. They refused, McWilliam left, and a long decline began. In 1927 Jimmy Seed also left the club for Sheffield Wednesday, inspiring them to two victories over Spurs which were to be instrumental in the London club's relegation. Seed went on to lead Wednesday to successive League titles while Spurs languished in Division Two for five seasons. Despite promotion in 1933 the team continued to struggle, finishing bottom two seasons later to begin a long exile from the top flight that was not ended until 1949. The most barren period in the club's history was about to give way to the most glorious.

Former player Arthur Rowe was the manager who led Spurs from the wilderness, implementing

a tactical style (see Tactics, page 115) that not only brought great success to Spurs, but revolutionised the world game. Rowe's 'push and run' team romped to promotion in 1949/50, leading the table from start to finish. The following year Spurs won their first League title, a 7-0 drubbing of a Newcastle United side featuring Milburn, Harvey and Robledo in the

Ron Burgess holds off Stanley Matthews during the 1948 FA Cup semi-final at Villa Park

November signalling the triumph of the new style over the traditional English approach. The team had some great players, Ron Burgess, Alf Ramsey, Eddie Baily and Ted Ditchburn among them, but its strength was as a unit and Spurs were widely acknowledged as the most thrilling and effective footballing machine in the land.

Creating one great team is achievement enough, but evolving to create another is a trickier challenge,

The Double secured, Danny Blanchflower and Bobby Smith parade the FA Cup at Wembley in 1961

'The team of the century': Tottenham Hotspur and the Double

and Rowe was unable to repeat his early success as his players grew older, injuries took their toll, and opponents began to close down the space Spurs needed to play. In 1955 Spurs were bottom of the table and Rowe, made ill by the pressure, stepped down. Before he did so he made one last major contribution – signing Danny Blanchflower.

Spurs avoided the drop and put together some good cup runs, but by 1958 manager Jimmy Anderson, Rowe's former assistant, was replaced by another former player – Bill Nicholson. Although Anderson never quite convinced either fans or directors, his signings – Bobby Smith, Maurice

Norman, Cliff Jones and Terry Dyson among them
– laid the foundations for Nicholson's success. To
this promising collection, Nicholson added Dave
Mackay, Bill Brown, John White and Les Allen. He
also recognised the genius of Blanchflower, as good a
football thinker as player, and made him his 'manager
on the pitch'.

In 1959/60 Spurs just missed out on another
League title after battling with the great Wolves and
Burnley sides of the time throughout the season.
But Blanchflower had seen enough to convince
him that Spurs could do the first Double in modern
football, and he told his chairman so at the start of
the campaign.

The team that achieved that historic feat in
1960/61 is still regarded as one of the finest
footballing units ever to take to a pitch. It set records
galore, including 11 wins in the first 11 games, and
played a style of football as aesthetically pleasing as
it was effective. It was the ultimate manifestation
of the close-passing, quick-moving, push-and-run
Spurs way. The title was secured at White Hart Lane,
Allen scoring the vital goal, after Spurs booked an
appearance at Wembley with an FA Cup semi-final
victory over Burnley. In the Final, Leicester were
beaten 2-0 thanks to goals from Smith and Dyson.
The Double, and a place in history, was secured.

Having conquered all domestically, the club's
attention turned to Europe. The European Cup
campaign of 1961/62 established the tradition of

White Hart Lane glory nights as Nicholson's Spurs gave some thrilling displays under floodlights against Europe's finest. They reached the semi-final, only to be edged out by the great Benfica side of the era. They retained the FA Cup, beating Burnley in the final, but

Ipswich – managed by former Spur Alf Ramsey – just beat them to the title and the Double Double. Key to the side's success that year was the signing of Jimmy Greaves – to many still the best natural goalscorer to grace the English game.

A handwritten sign proclaims the historic achievement as crowds greet the team outside the main gate at White Hart Lane

The cup win gave Spurs another crack at Europe, and in the 1962/63 Cup Winners' Cup they went all the way to the final in Rotterdam. Their opponents were Atletico Madrid, the holders and giants of the age. Spurs were given no chance, especially when Dave Mackay was ruled out through injury. But, roared on by the largest number of English supporters ever to travel to a European game, Spurs destroyed the Spaniards (see page 136) in a game in which Terry Dyson gave the performance of his life.

Spurs had done the Double, become the first British team to win a European trophy and changed the way the game was played. The success of 'the team of the century' reverberated far beyond the game itself. They were the first football superstars, blurring the lines between sport and showbusiness and in so doing they planted the seeds of a national fascination.

KIT PARADE

The famous white shirt has become so synonymous with Spurs that it inspires one of the club's most enduring nicknames, the Lilywhites. But the club did not wear white until 16 years after it was formed.

Spurs in 1884, influenced by Blackburn Rovers

Hotspur FC took to the field for their first game in 1882 clad in all navy. Two years later Tottenham adopted blue-and-white-halved shirts and white shorts, a choice made in honour of the Blackburn Rovers side which had won the FA Cup. The kit was commemorated in the club's 125th anniversary match in 2007, when the team took to the field against Aston Villa wearing an updated version.

In 1890, Spurs changed their shirt colour to red and the red shirts and blue shorts stayed until 1896. In that year, the club was elected to the Southern League and the club decided to mark the achievement by adopting a new kit which was described as "chocolate and gold". The striped shirts and dark shorts were worn for a further two seasons until, in 1898, a kit of white shirts, navy shorts and navy socks was adopted as a mark of respect for Preston North End, who played in those colours and were the dominant team of the age. Since then, the basics of the side's first team strip have remained virtually unchanged, another of the distinctive identifying symbols of the club alongside the cockerel and the name Hotspur.

In 1903 two white bands appeared around the top of the socks, and between 1911 and 1921 the bands merged to form a solid white block across the top of the socks. In the 1913/14 season the winged collar was made smaller and rounded and the number of buttons on the front was reduced. A badge appeared for the first time in 1921, a simple cockerel.

In 1937/38 the club's first change strip appeared, thick horizontal hoops in navy and white with navy shorts and navy socks with a white hoop. In the 1940s and 50s, two further change strips appeared. One was a vertically striped version of the hooped effort from 1937, the other comprised of a dark navy shirt with white contrast collar detail, white shorts and navy and white socks. This navy away shirt has become one of the most popular of the retro shirts currently being sold, probably

Chocolate and gold – an irresistible combination

The leader of the band
- Danny Blanchflower
and the Double shirt

because of the association with the years in which the club experienced its greatest successes.

In 1958 the first short-sleeved shirts appeared, and in 1959 the collar became a simple v-neck with no flaps. In 1964 the neck was made round, and featured as a contrast white band on the navy away shirt, which also had white cuffs.

The club's forays into Europe saw them wear an all-white strip, manager Bill Nicholson's nod to the Real Madrid side which dominated the early years of European competition. Spurs also wore all white in the 1967 FA Cup final.

In 1967, a yellow away shirt was worn for the first time. For three years this shirt went with navy shorts, with white shorts adopted between 1970 and 1975.

The first detail other than a badge to appear on a club shirt came in 1975, when kit maker Umbro's logo appeared on the shirt and shorts. This heralded a new era of huge change, in which the cult of the modern football kit grew. Over the next 34 years the club's shirts would feature stripes, bands, blocks, contrast stripes and patterns, eight different logos, chevrons, shaded sections, piping, collar detail, shorts panels, side panels, abstract patterns and contrast sleeves. While the first strip remained white and navy, change strips featured yellow, light blue, purple, navy, mauve and brown.

In 1986 a third kit was introduced, and the 125th anniversary was marked with four separate strips.

Yellow was the away colour between 1967 and 1982, at which point light blue took over. A purple and blue striped third kit appeared in 1986 and in 1995 the first yellow away shirt with blue sleeves was worn. The navy away shirt made a popular reappearance in 1997. In the 2005/06 season, the club made a significant change to the first team shirt for the first time in 107 years, adding blue sleeves to the white body.

In 1991, Spurs used the occasion of the first ever Wembley FA Cup semi-final to unveil a kit which featured longer, baggier shorts than had been the norm – another of the kit industry's seemingly endless innovations. The trend caught on and

Yellow was the colour for Martin Chivers and 70s Spurs away from home

thankfully for all concerned the tight shorties of the 80s are a thing of the past.

Holsten, the first sponsor's logo, appeared on shirts in 1983, an association that lasted until 1995. Since then Hewlett Packard, Thomson and Mansion have sponsored shirts. Umbro, Admiral, Le Coq Sportif, Hummel, Pony, Adidas, Kappa and Puma have all produced club kits.

Spurs produced their share of the eye-catching designs that graced playing fields in the 1980s and early 90s, with mention of these kits prompting affectionate good humour. In 1985, the addition of side chevrons on shirts and shorts, plus a row of chevrons running across the front of the shirt beneath a block of diagonal pinstripes, gave the impression of an explosion in a road sign factory. In 1991, the light blue third kit featured the word Spurs in six-inch high letters made from contrast pinstripes on a background of contrast

Jason Cundy shows off the early nineties' away kit

patterning; and 1994/95 saw the players run out in an abstract navy and purple graduated tint. The 1991–94 change kit, with its splash of blue zig-zags and squares planted jauntily on the right shoulder, retains a certain cult fascination.

Jermain Defoe in the 2009/10 home strip

Fans' favourites are the classic 50s and 60s home kits, the 1960s round-necked navy change shirt and the white home shirt of the early 80s with its v-neck and central cockerel and memories of Hoddle and Ardiles,.

Since 2006/07, Puma have manufactured Tottenham's kits, returning at first to relatively simple designs and clean lines. In 2007/08 the home kit was all-white – a nod to the kit adopted by Bill Nicholson's team in Europe. In 2009/10 yellow appeared on the home shirts for the first time, in an effort to combine the club's "three core colours". A panel beneath the crew-neck featured yellow edging from shoulder to mid-breast. The shirt also had yellow side panels, and splashes of yellow appeared on the shorts and socks.

HALL OF FAME

OSSIE ARDILES

"I fell in love with the club and it is still my favourite," says Ossie Ardiles today, and Tottenham's fans feel much the same way about him.

Ossie's arrival in a sensational £325,000 deal in July 1978 helped put newly-promoted Spurs back centre stage, and his skill and vision was a key factor in the moulding of one of the all-time great Spurs sides.

The sight of little Ardiles dancing through packed midfields, snapping off short passes and caressing longer balls accurately over distance fitted exactly the type of football Spurs fans value. A busy presence alongside Glenn Hoddle's grace, Ardiles linked the play expertly in the most creative midfield units in the club's history. "We played stylish football," says Ossie, "different to the rest of the country."

While Ardiles's technical abilities and reading of the game

are widely acknowledged, his toughness is often overlooked. Ardiles learned the game as a child in the streets of his home town where, as the smallest, he had to earn the right to play. His experience imbued a steely determination that would infuriate opponents who tried to muscle him out, and he loved scooting across the surface of heavy pitches with the ball at his feet.

ff This is a man's league. I don't think he'll last til Christmas JJ
Liverpool 'hard man' Tommy Smith in 1978

Tottenham's 1981 FA Cup final record *Ossie's Dream* immortalised his "trembley knees" but a more sombre note was struck the following season when the Argentine star was left out of the final because of the Falklands War. Thinking it unwise to return when the conflict finished, Ossie spent an unhappy loan period in Paris. Finally welcomed back to White Hart Lane, he broke his shin. A series of injuries were to disrupt the rest of his Spurs career.

In 1984 his introduction as a substitute in the UEFA Cup final proved pivotal, and in 1987 he regained his best form as part of David Pleat's five-man midfield but was ultimately to be disappointed as Spurs lost their first Wembley FA Cup final. He was transferred soon after, returning for a spell as manager in 1993.

Born: Cordoba, Argentina, 3rd August 1952
Spurs appearances: 385
Spurs goals: 37
Honours won with Spurs: FA Cup (1981), UEFA Cup (1984)
Other clubs: Instituto de Cordoba (1973), Belgrano (1974), Huracan (1975), PSG (1982), St George Saints (1982), Blackburn Rovers (1988), QPR (1988), Swindon Town (1989)
International appearances: Argentina, 63

OSSIE ARDILES FACTFILE

DANNY BLANCHFLOWER

Player, thinker, leader, visionary – Danny Blanchflower made his mark not just as a footballer but as a man.

Off the pitch, Danny had plenty to say, on it he let his actions do the talking. Intelligence ran through his comments on the game and his contributions to the games he played in – he was the independent who made the team of the century tick.

Signed from Aston Villa in 1954 for £30,000 by Arthur Rowe, he would forge one of the game's great relationships with the man he replaced, Bill Nicholson, when Nicholson became his manager. Rowe wanted Blanchflower for his ability but also his vision of how the game should be played. Blanchflower came to Spurs on a quest for glory that was to culminate in the historic Double of 1961.

He wasn't the quickest, or the toughest tackler, but his

ability to read the game, combined with technical prowess, enabled him to dictate play from the middle of the pitch. He needed the ball, and his team-mates gave it to him. "In nine matches out of ten, he's in possession more than any two players on the field put together," observed Rowe. He preferred to lead by example than through shouting and hollering and his calm manner was a real asset in high-pressure games. His ability to change the pace in an instant proved vital.

> **ff Football is about glory, it is about doing things in style, with a flourish, about going out and beating the other lot, not waiting for them to die of boredom JJ**
> Danny Blanchflower

At the start of the 1960/61 season, Blanchflower told his chairman "We'll do the Double this year." His vision and belief helped Spurs do so. In 1963 it's said he won the Cup Winners' Cup without playing because of the speech he gave beforehand in the dressing room.

Injury brought his career to a close in 1964 and he quit with regret but also the certainty that struggling on was not for him. He went on to forge a career in journalism, ever the man of words. And it is some words of his that still reverberate around White Hart Lane. "The game is about glory. It's about doing things in style."

He died after two years of debilitating illness in 1993.

DANNY BLANCHFLOWER FACTFILE

Born: Belfast, Northern Ireland, 10 February 1926
Spurs appearances: 436
Spurs goals: 27
Honours won with Spurs:
League title (1961), FA Cup (1961, 62), European Cup-Winners' Cup (1963)
Other clubs: Bloomeld United (1941), Glentoran (1942), Barnsley (1949), Aston Villa (1951)
International appearances:
Northern Ireland, 56

RON BURGESS

Described by Bill Nicholson as having all the requirements of the perfect footballer, Ron Burgess was the linchpin of the great push and run side and arguably established the modern tradition of the attacking half back.

Burgess learned to play on rough pitches alongside the pit slagheaps of the Rhondda Valley. He worked down the mine while playing for amateur side Cwm Villa, scoring 59 goals in one season. Spurs signed him in 1936, but after a year in London, he was told he wouldn't make the grade.

On his way home, Burgess stopped off to watch the A team play at White Hart Lane. They were a man short at right half, Burgess was drafted in, and history was made.

He made his debut in 1939 and by the time the League restarted after the war, Burgess was being acknowledged as the finest half back in the country after a series of international representative appearances.

Made captain in

1946, Burgess was the powerhouse of the Spurs team. He could tackle, head, pass, control the ball closely, read the game expertly and be a leader on the pitch. Deployed as a roving half back on the left, the right-footed Burgess would pick up short balls from the full backs to push on to the winger or inside left. He always said he had to curb his natural attacking instincts, but his defensive style was heavily offensive. This, together with his ability to organise and encourage his team-mates, was key in making manager Arthur Rowe's "keep it simple, keep it quick" maxim work as Spurs changed the tactical face of football.

" Captain and driving force of a Spurs team whose tactics ushered in an era of style and sophistication for English football "
The Times

Burgess led Spurs from the Second Division and, the following season, to their first League title and his phenomenal stamina saw him often labelled "the human dynamo". That he emerged as leader of a team that included Alf Ramsey and Bill Nicholson is testament to his qualities. In 1954 he left to become player-manager at Swansea Town. Later, as manager of Watford, he discovered Pat Jennings.

Burgess died in South Wales on 14th February 2005. He had said, "Soccer has been my life, my whole life, and I have no regrets."

Born: Cwm, Wales, 9th April 1917

Spurs appearances: 507

Spurs goals: 63

Honours won with Spurs: Second Division Championship (1950), League title (1951)

Other clubs: Swansea Town (1954)

International appearances: Wales, 32

RON BURGESS FACTFILE

PAUL GASCOIGNE

Midfielder Gascoigne was signed for a British record £2m in 1988 by Terry Venables. With Venables able to handle Gascoigne's ebullient personality in order to get the best out of him, Spurs fans saw three years of one of the most exciting talents in football at his best.

Gascoigne possessed the full set of skills, able to play passes perfectly, score and create goals, tackle and dribble at speed and, on the pitch, he never hid, always wanting the ball.

His petulance made people question his ability to handle pressure, but his liking for pranks endeared him to observers. He made his England debut a fortnight after signing for Spurs, and it was in the England shirt at the 1990 World Cup that he changed football forever. The image of him shedding tears after a semi-final booking is one of sport's most iconic, turning Gascoigne the footballer into Gazza the personality and football into a truly national obsession. The plastic boobs also helped.

The public spotlight put tremendous pressure on the 23-year-old and off-field problems grew. Gazza's only escape was on the pitch but, in 1991, he suffered a stomach injury. With the club's plan to sell their man to ease the financial crisis in doubt, FA Cup success was now essential. Gazza took the club to the final almost single-handedly with a series of outstanding performances. One month after an operation to fix his stomach muscles, he played the game of his life, scoring a superb free-kick against Arsenal in the Wembley semi-final and creating another goal before being substituted, exhausted.

The final was billed as Gazza's game but it proved to be a personal disaster as, hyped up, the midfielder committed two terrible fouls in the first 15 minutes. The second saw him carried off injured, lucky to escape a red card. The £8.5 million move to Lazio was delayed a year and, although Gascoigne eventually went, he was never the same player and his personal life descended into chaos.

Paul Gascoigne gave Spurs his best years, and played a key role in ensuring the club's survival. What more qualification does a legend need?

> **He's made mistakes in life but overall he's got a really good heart**
>
> Former team-mate Gary Lineker

Born: Gateshead, Tyne and Wear, 27th May 1967

Spurs appearances: 139

Spurs goals: 46

Honours won with Spurs: FA Cup (1991)

Other clubs: Newcastle United (1985), Lazio (1992), Glasgow Rangers (1995), Middlesbrough (1998), Everton (2000), Burnley (2002), Gansu Tainma (2003), Boston United (2004)

International appearances: England, 57

PAUL GASCOIGNE FACTFILE

JIMMY GREAVES

Tottenham Hotspur's greatest striker, and the best goalscorer in British football history. No contest.

Greaves was expected to sign for Spurs from school in 1955, but Arthur Rowe's illness allowed Chelsea to slip in. He made his debut against Spurs. And scored. After four electric years, Jimmy moved to AC Milan but, after an unhappy six months in Italy, was rescued by Bill Nicholson and finally arrived at Spurs. Signed for a record £99,999, he was the one player Nicholson thought would improve the Double side. Greaves scored a hat-trick on his debut, and went on to enjoy the best nine years of his career. In the 1962 FA Cup final he scored after three minutes, and a year later netted twice in Rotterdam as Spurs won the Cup Winners' Cup. He was top scorer in the top division three years running, racked up an astonishing two goals in every three games over the course of his career, and he scored on every top-class debut he made.

> **One of the best players the world has seen**
> Pele

In fact, all he did was score. He didn't tackle or chase much, he simply waited, weighing up the chances, until the opportunity came to pounce. His anticipation and razor-sharp reactions combined with lightening speed to make him almost unstoppable, and when he ran with the ball his balance and control were superb. He worked hard, always showing for the ball, alert to the angle or the space.

He would score by following shots into the box and nabbing the rebound, by turning and running into space or through packed defences, from distance and from close-range. He struck with precision and always made sure.

"Jim played football for fun," said team-mate Alan Mullery. "But unlike other players he was an absolute genius at it."

As the great team of the 1960s broke up, Greaves was transferred to West Ham as part of a swap deal for Martin Peters. He was heartbroken. In 1972 he became the first modern Spurs player to be granted a testimonial, and 45,799 turned out to honour him.

Born: East Ham, London, 20th February 1940
Spurs appearances: 420
Spurs goals: 306
Honours won with Spurs: FA Cup (1962, 67), European Cup-Winners' Cup (1963)
Other clubs: Chelsea (1957), AC Milan (1961), West Ham (1970), Brentwood Town (1975), Chelmsford City (1976), Barnet (1978)
International appearances: England, 57

JIMMY GREAVES FACTFILE

GLENN HODDLE

The cliché is that players "ooze" class. The player Spurs fans still revere dished it out with abandon.

He was, to employ an over-used but absolutely appropriate phrase, the most naturally-gifted player of his generation. A cultured, inventive midfielder, Hoddle embodied the finest traditions of the Spurs way, and was adored by the fans who chorused "Born is the King of White Hart Lane".

Hoddle signed for Spurs in 1975 and made his league debut in August. On his first full appearance in 1976 he beat England keeper Peter Shilton with a sweet long-range volley.

He could do anything with a ball, specialising in long-range passes delivered with perfect pace and accuracy. His poise and grace when dribbling was a joy to see. And he scored some great goals. When Spurs signed Ardiles and Villa in 1978, he gained the partners who would allow his outstanding skills to blossom, and together the trio formed the creative heart of an outstanding team. "Glenn was so good technically he could even put backspin on a pass," remembers winger Tony Galvin.

Success at Wembley and in Europe followed, with manager Keith Burkinshaw picking out Hoddle's performance in the 1981 Cup final as one of his best – a performance in which the work ethic Hoddle was frequently criticised for lacking shone through. In 1984 he humbled Dutch legend Johan Cruyff in a UEFA Cup second round match against Feyenoord, Cruyff conceding after the game, "I was a shadow without any presence."

Later, under David Pleat, Hoddle played as an attacking midfielder roaming behind lone striker Clive Allen and alongside wide man Chris Waddle.

In 1987, he left for a new challenge in the French League, signing off with a beauty of a goal at White Hart Lane.

He went on to forge a successful managerial career at club and international level and, when he arrived to take the reins at Spurs in 2001, expectation was high. But things didn't work out.

Hoddle now runs a football academy and is a regular pundit when Spurs are live on TV.

> **❝ Why have they signed us? They have him! ❞**
> Ricky Villa to Ossie Ardiles upon first seeing Hoddle train

Born: Hayes, Middlesex, 27th October 1957

Spurs appearances: 566

Spurs goals: 132

Honours won with Spurs: FA Cup (1981, 82), UEFA Cup (1984)

Other clubs: As Monaco (1987), Swindon Town (1991), Chelsea (1993)

International appearances: England, 53

GLENN HODDLE FACTFILE

PAT JENNINGS

Rivalled only by Ted Ditchburn as Spurs' greatest goalkeeper, and hailed as the world's No 1 during his career, Jennings is a true giant.

At 6ft and in possession of enormous hands, he pioneered the practice of standing up instead of diving early. He reasoned there was more chance of making a save from a standing position, and also defied accepted wisdom by sticking out a foot to deflect balls close to him in order to reduce the risk of them creeping under his body. His unorthodox approach was based on his early years playing Gaelic football.

Jennings dominated his area, using feet, legs and those huge hands to keep the ball out. He once saved two penalties in one game, against Liverpool in front of The Kop, and even scored in the Charity Shield.

When he arrived in 1964 he was barracked by fans who didn't think he filled Bill Brown's boots, and Bill Nicholson had to appeal for his new signing to be given a chance. The arrival of centre back Mike England also helped boost Jennings's confidence. In the 1967 FA Cup final he was superb, reaching to pluck a dangerous cross from the air in the dying minutes with one hand in what was to become a trademark action.

" I was certain it was in... then this massive great hand appeared as if from nowhere to flick the ball over the bar "
Liverpool's Ian Callaghan recalls being frustrated by Big Pat

He was voted Footballer of the Year by the football writers in 1973 and by his peers in 1976, when he was also awarded an MBE. That year he also suffered his first real injury, which led eventually to his sale to Arsenal. Keith Burkinshaw thought Pat's best years were behind him, a view he has since acknowledged was a mistake.

Pat returned to Spurs in 1985 to keep fit for the World Cup finals – he still holds a record 119 caps for Northern Ireland. He went on to become a goalkeeping coach for the club, and currently works as a match day host at White Hart Lane. Quietly-spoken Pat holds the rare distinction of being popular with fans of both Spurs and Arsenal.

Born: Newry, Northern Ireland, 12th June 1945
Spurs appearances: 673
Spurs goals: 1
Honours won with Spurs: FA Cup (1967), League Cup (1971, 73), UEFA Cup (1972)
Other clubs: Newry Town (1961), Watford (1963), Arsenal (1977)
International appearances: Northern Ireland, 119

PAT JENNINGS FACTFILE

CLIFF JONES

Pace, vision, skill and bravery were the qualities which made winger Cliff Jones one of the key members of Bill Nicholson's 'Team of the Century'.

Adept with either foot, the naturally right-footed winger made his name on the left wing, cutting inside opponents at speed to create havoc. Given freedom to roam by Nicholson, Jones was as good at scoring goals as he was at setting them up, and he specialised in headed goals, timing his runs from the wing perfectly to fling himself into the thick of things in the box. A potent attacking threat, Jones also had the brains and ability to hold the ball up on the flanks when his team-mates tired, his seemingly adhesive first-touch bewildering opponents.

Jones's speed and ability meant he took a lot of punishment – sometimes from mistimed challenges, more often from attempts to kick him out of the game. However badly he was clattered, Jones would simply pick himself up, dust himself down, and carry on. Extraordinarily he would leave his shinpads in the dressing room, saying they slowed him down. Nicholson called him "enormously brave".

> **The lithe Welshman seems to skim the surface as he glides past opponents**
> Team-mate Dave Mackay

Signed for £35,000 in 1957 from Swansea Town, Jones scored 20 goals in 38 games in his first full season – some achievement for a winger. The next year he got 25 in 42. In the Double season he contributed 19 goals in League and FA Cup. Atletico Madrid and Juventus offered big money for him, but Nicholson said he was priceless. In Spurs' first home tie in Europe in 1962, Jones scored the perfect hat-trick – right foot, left foot, header – as Gornik Zabre were trounced 8-1. In the 1963 Cup Winners' Cup final he set up the first two goals and ran Atletico ragged. In 1967 he became the first substitute in an FA Cup final to collect a winners' medal.

A lovely man as well as a great footballer, club favourite Jones was allowed to leave for Fulham on a cut-price transfer in 1969. He signed off by scoring against Manchester United.

Born: Swansea, Wales, 7th February 1935

Spurs appearances: 408

Spurs goals: 174

Honours won with Spurs: League Championship (1961), FA Cup (1961, 62, 67), European Cup-Winners' Cup (1963)

Other clubs: Swansea Town (1952), Fulham (1969), Kings Lynn (1970)

International appearances: Wales, 59

CLIFF JONES FACTFILE

DAVE MACKAY

For many, the greatest Spur ever. Mackay is remembered as a hard man, but he was no mere destroyer.

He could control and pass a ball expertly and, while his tackling and work rate caught the eye, he could score with the most delicate of chips. And his utter determination meant the fans took to him from the start.

When he signed from Hearts in 1959 for £30,000, Mackay had already won every honour in Scottish football. His arrival at Spurs turned a good team into a great one. His presence in the centre of midfield freed Danny Blanchflower's creative talents, and gave winger Cliff Jones the opportunity to show his full potential. Jimmy Greaves said only Bobby Moore matched up to Mackay in his ability to control the ball in tight situations or to make a first-time pass.

He hardly missed a game during the Double season, was a leading force as Spurs retained the FA Cup the following year, and powered the drive to the Cup Winners' Cup final in 1963. But injury forced him to miss the final, leaving even Bill Nicholson to doubt his team's chances.

> ** He was the best professional I ever played alongside **
> Jimmy Greaves

Spurs won but, the following season, the same competition proved to be doubly unlucky for Mackay. In their first game as holders, Spurs met Manchester United and Mackay suffered a broken leg that kept him out for the season. "The heart of the Double side went with him," said Jimmy Greaves. "We were never the same again."

A year later, in his comeback match for the reserves, Mackay's leg was broken again. For most players, two breaks would have ended their career. Not Dave. After another year out, Mackay returned to the first team, a little slower and now playing at the back, but more inspirational than ever. He'd taken over the captaincy from Blanchflower, and everyone knew who was boss on the pitch.

He led Spurs to a remarkable third FA Cup in six years in 1967 before being released in 1968 to Derby County. Bill Nicholson told Joe Kinnear, "I'll never find another Dave Mackay."

Born: Musselburgh, Scotland, 13th November 1934

Spurs appearances: 362
Spurs goals: 63

Honours won with Spurs: League title (1961), FA Cup, (1961, 62, 67)

Other clubs: Hearts (1953), Derby County (1968), Swindon Town (1971)

International appearances: Scotland, 22

DAVE MACKAY FACTFILE

STEVE PERRYMAN

Steve Perryman's record number of appearances for Spurs and his qualities as a captain are what tend to be brought up most often, but he was also a far more gifted player than is generally acknowledged.

He was the foundation upon which four successive teams were built in a career lasting from 1969 to 1986.

Signed straight from school, Perryman made his debut at 17 in 1969 in midfield. By 1971 he was lifting the first of six trophies and, by 1973, was appointed the club's youngest ever captain.

His brief was to break up opposition attacks in midfield, and in his early days he matched legendary hard men Tommy Smith and Johnny Giles in every tackle. But he was also a gifted playmaker, able to control the ball and lay off passes at the right time.

As Spurs went into decline in the mid-1970s, Perryman had to concentrate more on the defensive side of his game, a source of some regret, but never an excuse to do anything but his best.

Under Keith Burkinshaw, Perryman moved to central defence, his vision and shrewdness making up for his lack of inches. Personally affronted when Spurs went down in 1977, he led his team straight back into the top flight.

The switch to full back the following season ushered in the best spell of his career, and one of the best in Tottenham's history. Steve says, "All I had to do was give the ball to Glenn Hoddle," but his constant darts forward and defensive qualities were vital.

He captained the side to FA Cup glory twice and, such was the esteem in which he was held by his team-mates, received his great friend Ossie Ardiles's UEFA Cup winners' medal in 1984 despite being suspended. He was awarded the MBE in 1986, the year he left Spurs.

He returned in 1993 as Ossie Ardiles's assistant for a short spell, and is now Director of Football at Exeter City.

> ** The most loyal player in the club's history **
> THFC official website

STEVE PERRYMAN FACTFILE

Born: Ealing, London, 21st December 1951

Spurs appearances: 1014

Spurs goals: 51

Honours won with Spurs: League Cup (1971, 73), FA Cup (1981, 82), UEFA Cup (1972, 84)

Other clubs: Oxford United (1986), Brentford (1987)

International appearances: England, 1

SPURS IN EUROPE

The European stage is one Spurs have relished over the years since they first took on the Continent's finest in 1962/63. When Spurs entered the European Cup that year, only three English teams had done so before – Wolves, Burnley and Manchester United.

In the 49 years since, some of the greatest teams and players in the history of the European game have graced White Hart Lane – Eusebio and Benfica, Rivera of AC Milan, Cruyff in his Feyenoord days, Bayern Munich and Karl Heinz Rumminegge and Real Madrid and Emilio Butragueno.

The adventure started in the heart of Poland's mining country, where a crowd of 90,000 provided passionate backing for their side Gornik Zabre. The number in the away contingent for a trip that was almost impossible to negotiate in 1962 is uncertain, but it may have been as low as one. According to the *Daily Mail*, only "a nomadic Southampton student named David Mummery" was there to fly the flag.

Spurs lost 4-2, but the second leg gave birth to the tradition of raw, emotional, gripping occasions which came to define the glory nights that are so deeply associated with the club. According to the *Daily Express*: "Eleven men playing flawless football with the determination of giants who will not be beaten" destroyed the Poles 8-1. Those who were there say they will never forget the wall of sound with which the home crowd greeted the teams and continued to roar on the Spurs.

The adventure ended on, inevitably, a night of high emotion at White Hart Lane against the great Benfica side of Bela Guttmann which featured the legendary Eusebio. Spurs lost the semi-final 4-3 on aggregate and Jimmy Greaves was controversially denied a goal 23 minutes into the second leg at home which could have forced a replay. It was one of the finest games ever seen in European football, but good as Spurs were, and controversial as that disallowed goal was, no one could deny the quality of the Benfica side which went on to lift the trophy.

Danny Blanchlower shakes hands with Benfica captain Jose Aguas before the epic 1962 match

But Spurs had learned lessons. "We were no longer the innocents abroad", said Greaves. In the next season they reached the final in the Cup-Winners' Cup. Glasgow Rangers were swept aside 8-4 on aggregate in a titanic opening round Battle of Britain, Slovan Bratislava had six thumped past them in London as Spurs won 6-2 on aggregate and OFK Belgrade were despatched 5-2.

Despite the thrilling run, Spurs entered the final in Rotterdam as underdogs. Their opponents were Atletico Madrid, the holders and one of the finest teams in Europe. By the end of the night Spurs were the new masters, roared on by nearly 4,000 fans, the largest number ever to travel

to Europe from England to watch their team. Spurs became the first British side to win a European trophy. The full story of that famous 5-1 win can be found in the Great Games section.

Spurs went out of the same competition in the first round the following season, knocked out by Manchester United in a game in which Dave Mackay broke his leg. Bill Nicholson's greatest team was breaking up and it would be 1967 before Spurs were back in Europe, once again in the Cup-Winners' Cup. In the second round Spurs went out to Lyon on away goals after a stormy first

The two heroes of a glorious 1984 night, goal scorer Graham Roberts and goal-stopper Tony Parks

leg in France that was dubbed The Battle of Lyon.

In 1971, Spurs were in the newly-named UEFA Cup and racked up what is still their record European victory in the first round. Icelandic part-timers Kelflavik were the opponents, 15-1 the aggregate score. A semi-final victory over a gifted but physical AC Milan side in which two-volleyed goals from Steve Perryman proved vital secured Spurs their second European final. Against Wolves!

A trip to Birmingham did not, evidently, go down well with the wives, but players and fans were delighted when Spurs won the Cup at White Hart Lane. Alan Mullery's headed goals added to two fine first-leg strikes from Martin Chivers to secure a 3-2 victory. It seemed to be more of the same as Spurs started their defence of the trophy with a 12-3 aggregate victory over Lyn Oslo, but Liverpool proved too tough to overcome in the semi-final.

In 1974 Spurs again reached the final of the UEFA Cup, with victory over Cologne the pick of some fine performances. But the final was lost as Spurs made an unhappy return to Rotterdam, Feyenoord winning in a second leg scarred by terrible rioting on the terraces.

It was ten years before Spurs returned to Europe, this time in the Cup-Winners' Cup. The team of Hoddle, Crooks and Ardiles reached the semi-final, only to be kicked out by a brutal Barcelona side. But the following year brought Tottenham's third European trophy, the route to the final lit considerably by a tie in which Hoddle played the great Johan Cruyff off the White Hart Lane pitch. In the final against Anderlecht, a nail-biting night in north London saw Tony Parks' heroics in goal help Spurs win a penalty shootout to lift the trophy.

Real Madrid put Spurs out in the fourth round of the following season's competition, and it would be 1991 before Spurs were back in Europe. Feyenoord again proved too much for Spurs in the Cup-Winners' Cup, winning a third round tie. In 1999 Spurs went out of the UEFA Cup in the second round after being minutes from beating Kaiserslautern, and in the same competition in 2006 Seville proved too strong in the quarter-finals.

A proud record went the following year when Spurs lost their first-ever European home tie, against Getafe in the group stage. They eventually went out on penalties to PSV Eindhoven in the third round. And in 2009 eventual winners Shakhtar Donetsk won 3-1 over two second round legs.

IF YOU KNOW YOUR HISTORY
UPS AND DOWN
1964-77

After a historic few seasons in which Spurs set new standards, Bill Nicholson was faced with the task of rebuilding his great team. Mackay, indisputably the leader now Blanchflower had played his last game, was sidelined for two years with a broken leg. And in the summer of 1964, genuine tragedy struck when John White, a gifted inside forward who was key to Nicholson's rebuilding plans, was killed by lightning on a golf course. It was to be four years before the team had a trophy in its sights again.

In the 1966/67 season, Spurs were top of the table in October, but slumped badly to leave the title a distant dream. This left the FA Cup as the sole focus and Spurs reached Wembley to face Chelsea in the first all-London final, and their fifth.

The Cockney Cup final was billed as a clash of styles, Tottenham's measured close-passing game against the bustling, hard-running style of Tommy Docherty's Blues. In the end, it was no contest. Spurs dominated the 90 minutes with a display of elegance and style, rarely letting Chelsea get a look in. Mike England shut out Chelsea's one attacking threat, Tony Hateley, while Alan Gilzean and Jimmy Greaves led Chelsea's defence a dance and Alan Mullery's marauding runs from deep provided yet another option. Goals from Jimmy Robertson and Frank Saul secured a 2-1 win, and Dave Mackay lifted the cup to complete the achievement of playing in three FA Cup-winning sides in seven years.

Spurs were back in Europe the following season, but an early exit after a controversial clash with Olympique Lyonnaise only heightened the sense of disappointment. Nothing measured up to the achievements of the Double side and Spurs, despite their reputation, were also not attracting the young players needed to build a new dynasty. This was partly due to tax rules which led Spurs to spend big on transfers in order to reduce profits and cut corporation tax. Of the side that won the Cup in

(From left) Alan Mullery, Dave Mackay and Jimmy Robertson lead the celebrations after the 1967 FA Cup final

1967, only two players were home-grown. Building a consistent team from a constantly changing cast was difficult. Football was also changing, with avoiding defeat becoming more important than winning with style, and Nicholson was not prepared to sacrifice his principles.

In January 1970 a limited but committed Crystal

Palace knocked Spurs out of the FA Cup. Nicholson responded by axing a number of established stars. Greaves was offloaded to West Ham in exchange for Martin Peters. A new era had begun, one in which Spurs were to firmly establish their reputation as a cup team.

In 1970/71 Spurs reached the League Cup final, a competition they had at first shunned but was now made more attractive by the prospect of a European place for the winners. Opponents Aston Villa were in the Third Division, but third-tier teams had beaten top-flight opponents in the competition's final twice before, and Spurs knew they would have to compete hard. Villa soaked up Tottenham's early dominance and began to push on, prompting sterling performances from Steve Perryman and Phil Beal as Spurs struggled to hold the line. In the end, two goals from Martin Chivers, the country's finest centre forward, settled the contest and Spurs had another trophy.

That same season saw Spurs finish third in the League and reach the quarter-final of the FA Cup. It also signalled the start of a remarkable run of

(From left) Martin Chivers, Bill Nicholson and Alan Mullery lift the 1971 League Cup

Alan Mullery heads
the goal against Wolves
that won the 1972 UEFA
Cup as a packed
Shelf Side looks on

four finals in four seasons. In 1971/72
Spurs's indifferent league form provided
a contrast to their progress in the first
UEFA Cup, a campaign which stared
with a 15-1 aggregate demolition of
Icelandic minnows Keflavik. The semi-
final threw up an almighty clash with
AC Milan. Spurs won the first leg 2-1,
thanks to a brace from the unlikely
figure of Perryman. The return at the
San Siro was an ugly affair, with Milan
defensive and niggly, but Mullery's fine
performance helped secure a 1-1 draw
and a place in the final.

It was to be an all-English affair
against Wolves, and the first leg at
Molineux is remembered best for the
stunning second goal scored by Chivers
to give Spurs a 2-1 lead.

In the second, an exhausted Spurs
held on for a 1-1 draw. Mullery,
playing his last game for the club,
scored the goal and did a lone lap of
honour in the midst of 4,000 delirious
fans who joined him on the pitch. The season
was also the subject of Hunter Davies's classic book
The Glory Game.

While the decline in League performances
continued in 1972/73, Spurs reached their second
League Cup final, this time beating Norwich City

in a mediocre game. A goal from Ralph Coates gave
Spurs their ninth win in nine finals, and another
European campaign. In that following season Spurs
struggled in the League and went out of both
domestic cups at the first attempt. Only the UEFA

Cup provided cheer, Spurs reaching the final against Feyenoord. A 2–2 in the home leg gave Spurs a tough task, and the return to Rotterdam could not have been more different to the joyous visit in 1963. Spurs lost amidst terrible scenes of rioting on the terraces of the De Kuip stadium.

It was a turning point. Spurs had lost their first final and Nicholson was disillusioned by the game and sickened by the violence he had appealed in vain to stop. After four straight defeats the following season, he resigned. The directors simply waved the club's greatest manager on his way, and ignored his recommendation that Blanchflower succeed him. Instead, former Arsenal captain Terry Neill was appointed. Spurs just stayed up that season, but the following campaign was disrupted when Neill quit… to manage Arsenal!

Keith Burkinshaw, a club coach who had the support of the players, replaced him but the team simply was not good enough and, in 1976/77, Spurs finished bottom of the First Division. A 26-year stint in the top flight was over.

Bright young hope Glenn Hoddle in action against Manchester United in 1977

SPURS COMIC STRIP HISTORY

3

IN A LEAGUE MATCH AT THE EMIRATES STADIUM IN 2008, DAVID BENTLEY GAVE SPURS AN EARLY LEAD WITH A SPECTACULAR LONG-DISTANCE STRIKE, BUT TO THE DISMAY OF NEW MANAGER HARRY REDKNAPP, ARSENAL TURNED THE TABLES...

4-2! WE'VE WON IT NOW!

I DON'T BELIEVE IT...

THERE WERE JUST TWO MINUTES TO GO, BUT...

JENAS HAS SCORED!

WHAT THE..?

IT'S 4-3!

SPURS!

THEN, IN THE LAST MINUTE OF ADDED TIME, AARON LENNON WAS IN THE RIGHT PLACE TO PICK UP A REBOUND...

4-4!

GET IN MY SON! YOU *BEAUTY!*

ARSENAL HAD BEEN MUGGED!

TACTICS

BILL NICHOLSON'S PUSH AND RUN

In 1949, Tottenham boss Arthur Rowe combined the club's traditional passing game with ideas he had developed as a coach in Hungary, and in the process revolutionised the English game.

Rowe reasoned that the shorter the pass, the less likely the opposition were to intercept; and the greater the movement of players off the ball, the more opportunities would be created. The 'push and run' system produced flowing, exhilarating football. In 1951, *The Telegraph* described it as "like a wave gathering momentum", adding: "It is all worked out in triangles and squares and when the mechanism clicks… there is simply no defence against it."

Ten years later Bill Nicholson's team took the style to its ultimate expression by securing the first modern Double. Nicholson's 1961 formation was the solid W-M which had dominated the game since the 1930s, but with the application of push and run to emphasise movement and possession.

The key to the tactics of the Double team was Dave Mackay. His bravery, intelligence and fierce competiveness in the middle of the pitch alongside Danny Blanchflower gave the Irishman the opportunity to orchestrate the play, a task he performed superbly. All five forwards, Bobby Smith, Terry Dyson, Cliff Jones, Les Allen and John White, reached double figures before the season's halfway stage, emphasising the options the team had. Maurice Norman was commanding in the air at the back, Peter Baker and Ron Henry impassable either side and canny going forward.

It was, says football writer Julie Welch, "the greatest footballing machine there has ever been."

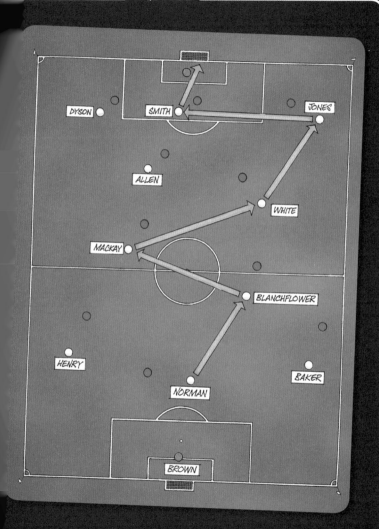

GENERAL BURKINSHAW'S ARMY

Yorkshireman Keith Burkinshaw created a team with flair and beauty at its heart and in so doing won more trophies than any Spurs manager except Bill Nicholson.

Essentially a 4-4-2, his team of the early 1980s featured such a wealth of creative talent that a rigid structural description barely does it justice. At its heart was Glenn Hoddle, able to create or score and one of the best passers of the ball the game has seen. Alongside him Ossie Ardiles, skilful and intelligent, linked the play and skipped through opposing defences. Ricky Villa preferred a central role, but with Ardiles and Hoddle playing there he was often stationed out wide, from where he would terrorise defences by running at them, often drifting inside. On the opposite side, Tony Galvin bossed the wing. Up front the partnership between Steve Archibald and Garth Crooks clicked straight away. Archibald was the artist, leading the line with a fine touch and unshakeable determination, while the livewire Crooks's movement and touch bamboozled defences allowing him a trademark opportunist strike or a set-up for Archibald.

At full back, Steve Perryman and Chris Hughton knew how to tackle, but Hughton especially pushed up so often he was almost an extra winger. Graham Roberts and Paul Miller in central defence were a formidable pairing – and needed to be.

A favourite move saw Perryman take the ball short from the goalkeeper and shape to burst down the right. Instead, he'd slip the ball inside to Hoddle, whose pinpoint long pass to Galvin bombing forward on the wing would unlock many a defence.

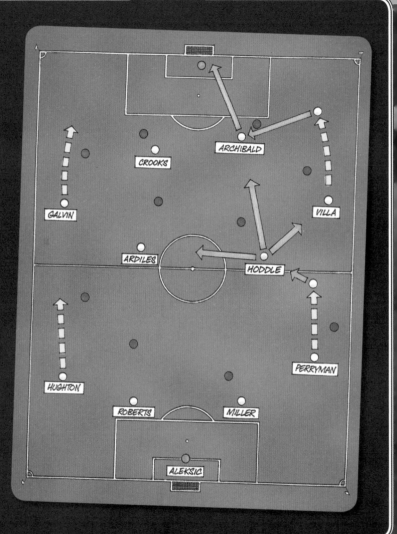

GALVIN
CROOKS
ARCHIBALD
VILLA
ARDILES
HODDLE
HUGHTON
PERRYMAN
ROBERTS
MILLER
ALEKSIC

ARDILES'S FAMOUS FIVE

Widely ridiculed as naïve when introduced in 1994, Ossie Ardiles's 'famous five' formation does not look quite so unlikely these days. Back then, it was portrayed as 'five up front' by a game in thrall to the 4-4-2, but now it would be understood as the kind of fluid 4-1-3-2 favoured by top European teams.

In many ways the formation was forced upon Ardiles. He had five supremely skilful attacking players; Jurgen Klinsmann and Teddy Sheringham were two of the finest strikers in the world, Ilie Dumitescu was a technically gifted World Cup star and Nick Barmby and Darren Anderton two of the English game's most exciting talents. They were all capable of superb creative football in the Tottenham tradition. Unfortunately, for such an attacking line-up to work, the defence needed to play its part and, to be frank, it was not up to the job.

Colin Calderwood was a decent player, but not the kind of commanding midfield general who would emerge as a key part of the top teams of the late 1990s. The full backs needed to be athletic, canny and technically gifted, but Justin Edinburgh – while committed – did not fit the bill and neither did David Kerslake. In central defence, Sol Campbell was not yet the commanding figure he would become, and Stuart Nethercott never was.

With a defensive unit incapable of breaking up opposition attacks and unable to unlock the attacking flair the side had, Ardiles's team was easily overwhelmed. He still maintains, with some justification, that he had little choice but to play this formation, and looked at from today's perspective it could fairly be argued that it was not the formation but the personnel that proved Ardiles's undoing.

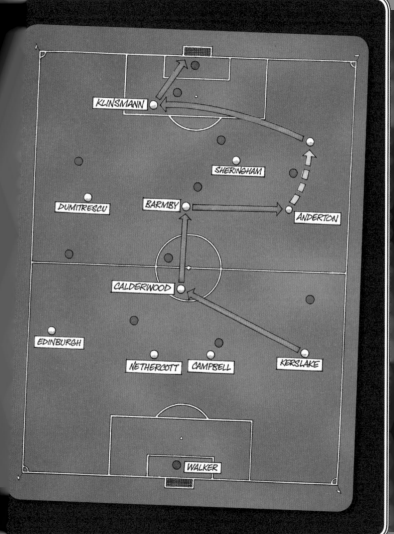

KLINSMANN

SHERINGHAM

DUMITRESCU

BARMBY

ANDERTON

CALDERWOOD

EDINBURGH

NETHERCOTT

CAMPBELL

KERSLAKE

WALKER

REDKNAPP'S 4-4-2

Not only did Tottenham Hotspur achieve a place in the Champions League for the first time under the guidance of an English manager, they did so by playing a game based on a formation synonymous with the traditional English approach – 4-4-2, and with a core of young, English players.

This observation is not to encourage insularity, rather to say that it can sometimes be productive to reassess traditional virtues. Key to Redknapp's successful tenure has been a tendency to keep things uncomplicated, and it's from a simple base that Spurs have created some thrilling football.

What's also worth mentioning is that, while the line-up shown is arguably the 2009/10 season's strongest 11, the players rarely turned out like this. The other vital factor in Tottenham's success was the ability of players to step in and more than do a job; Bassong for King, Bentley for Lennon, Palacios for Huddlestone, Kranjcar for Bale, Payluchenko for Defoe – this was truely a squad success.

Most eye-catching was the wing play of England's Lennon and Wales's Bale; two quick, technically adept wingers who take on defenders and can hit the by-line to produce a cross or cut in to have a crack at goal. In the middle, Croatian Luka Modric displays his fine footballing brain, coming deep to build the play or slotting neat passes forward. Alongside England's Tom Huddlestone he formed one of the best passing partnerships in the country.

Two strong, ball-playing central defenders and a genuinely world class goalkeeper kept it tight at the back, with the full backs not afraid to sally forward. And up front, Defoe's poacher's instinct and Crouch's ability to hold up the play completed the picture.

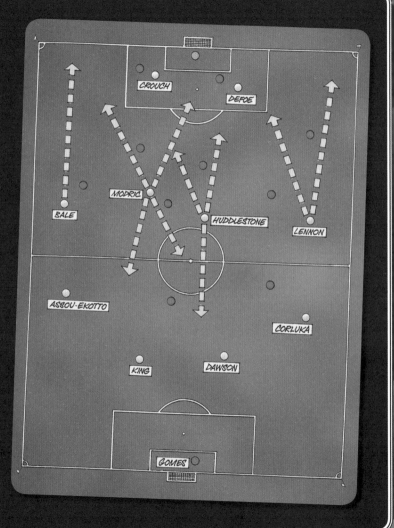

GREAT
GAFFERS

A large proportion of the club's managers have been influential not only in the progress of Tottenham Hotspur, but also on the development of the game itself. One such towering figure was John Cameron, who held the roles of player, secretary and manager – all three at once for a while – between 1899 and 1907.

Player, club secretary, manager – John Cameron was an early inspiration

Cameron had been a distinguished inside forward with Spurs, and eagerly took on the role of secretary manager when the previous incumbent Frank Brettell resigned in February 1899. Cameron led Spurs to the Southern League Championship in 1900 and the famous FA Cup win a year later. In 1903/04 he led Spurs to the London League title and by now was effectively running the club day-to-day.

He had a talent for administration and an enviable set of contacts, thanks largely to his efforts to establish the first footballers' union. He insisted that Spurs play the fast attacking football developed in the club's early years, a style for which the club has always striven. He was one of the first regular football columnists, called upon regularly to write in the newspapers on the burning topics of the day.

In 1906 the directors decided his burden was too

great and appointed Arthur Turner as club secretary.
Stories began to circulate of "differences" between
Cameron and the board and in 1907 the first 'Mr
Tottenham' suddenly resigned. Like another club
great in later years, Cameron took to journalism after
he quit the game, and wrote the first history of Spurs,
*The White Hart's Souvenir of the Spurs Entry to the
English League*, in 1908.

The next manager to make a significant impression
was Arthur Rowe, who took the reins from 1949 to
1955. Rowe was born close to White Hart Lane, had
been a boyhood Spurs fan, and
was a distinguished centre
half for the club
between 1930 and
1939. After hanging up
his boots he lectured in
Hungary, making a
strong impression on
Gusztav Sebes, who

A studious Arthur Rowe
at his desk in 1950

Bill Nicholson, Mr
Tottenham Hotspur

went on to coach the famous Magical Magyars national side of the early 1950s.

The Hungarian government actually offered Rowe the job of coaching their amateur team for the Helsinki Olympics in 1940, but the outbreak of war meant he stayed in England, where his ideas revolutionised the game. He saw keeping possession as key, and pioneered a combination of passing and movement known as push and run. It was simple, effective and a joy to watch.

His team won the Second Division title in 1949/50 and the First Division title 12 months later. There were some outstanding individuals on show; Ron Burgess, Eddie Baily, Ted Ditchburn and Alf Ramsey among them. But while the team's strength was in the way it operated as a unit, its fortunes also began to decline as those individuals aged.

In 1955, the pressure of trying to match his greatest achievement took its toll and Rowe resigned, 13 months after suffering a breakdown. Typically, he resigned for the good of the club. One of his final acts was to sign a certain Danny Blanchflower.

The man whose name will forever be synonymous with Tottenham's glory became manager in 1958. Bill Nicholson had played in Rowe's great team, and had a similarly lengthy association with Spurs. His first game in charge was won 10-4, but it was a tough first season as Spurs flirted with relegation. But in his first full season Spurs finished third and the following year achieved immortality by doing the first modern Double. Under Nicholson Spurs enjoyed their greatest days. They won four trophies in three years, including the first European trophy won by a British team, and they did it by playing thrilling, entertaining football. Some who witnessed his team at the height of its powers still call it the greatest football machine ever to take the field.

Bill and his team celebrate the Double

Having set new standards for football, Nicholson went on to successfully rebuild his team not once, but twice. Spurs won the FA Cup in 1967, then three more trophies, including the first UEFA Cup, between 1971 and 1973. He was uncompromising in his principles about how the game should be played and in what was best for Spurs. But his players loved him.

Nicholson took Rowe's push and run onto the next level, injecting some steel but still emphasising pass and move and entertain. Faced with another rebuilding job in 1974, unwilling to embrace the negative tactics that were becoming prevalent in the game and sickened by the violence on the terraces in Rotterdam as Spurs lost the UEFA Cup final, he resigned.

Spurs were relegated in Keith Burkinshaw's first full season in charge, 1976/77. But the board stuck by him and, in return, Burkinshaw went on to win more trophies than any manager except Nicholson. He engineered a return to the top flight at the first attempt, built a team around the talents of Glenn Hoddle – a feat no England manager even tried – and scooped the world to sign two Argentine World Cup stars. Working closely with Peter Shreeve, he was one of the first coaches to introduce psychological training and nutritional science, but his no-nonsense style placed him firmly in the Nicholson mould – a manager respected and loved by his players.

Keith Burkinshaw says farewell with his leaving present, the 1984 UEFA Cup

Two FA Cups, a UEFA Cup and the club's first

serious title challenge for years – plus an iron adherence to the traditional attacking style – made Burkinshaw a club great but, in 1984, he resigned citing differences with then club chairman Irving Scholar.

Harry Redknapp, Barclays Manager of the Season in 2009/10

Current manager Harry Redknapp deserves mention for taking Spurs to their highest finish in the Premiership, particularly as this saw the team score the highest number of goals since 1992/93. The feat is all the more remarkable considering that, when he arrived less than two seasons before the club was bottom of the table.

Redknapp's team plays attractive football thanks to some exciting talents, but also to his abilities to motivate the players and create a good spirit. As journalist Patrick Barclay says, "He is astute enough to know what a player can do and enough of a psychologist to get him to do it."

Now Redknapp. like everyone at Spurs, is relishing the chance for a crack at the Champions League.

MEMORABLE
MATCHES

SPURS 2 SHEFFIELD UNITED 2

FA Cup final, Crystal Palace, 20th April 1901

This clash of north v south drew a then world-record crowd of 114,815 to the south London suburb of Sydenham on a bright Spring day.

The non-League side immortalised on a cigarette card

Spurs were the first club from London and the first with mass working class support to reach the FA Cup final, already the highlight of the season, and this was a symbolic clash in many ways. The rising force of southern non-League football was pitted against the giants of the northern-dominated Football League, and London pride burned to break the Football League's monopoly of the cup. It was, quite simply, the biggest cup final attraction of all time.

United were the favourites, a team packed with big stars – none bigger than 6ft 2in, 21 stone goalkeeper Billy 'Fatty' Foulke – and dominated the early stages, Fred Priest putting them one up after 12 minutes. But the Spurs defence held firm in the face of sustained attack, and on the half hour Sandy Brown rose to head home a free kick to level the score. The game became more intense, but the Londoners' close passing began to open up United's defence. On 50 minutes, Brown got a second.

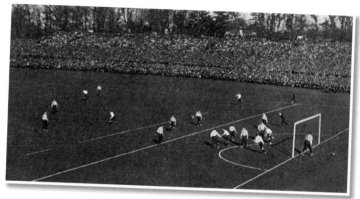

Spurs were ahead. Hundreds of hats sailed into the air and thousands of handkerchiefs fluttered as Tottenham's jubilant fans celebrated.

Spurs score in the final as the vast crowd looks on from packed banks

Just one minute later, however, the scores were levelled in controversial circumstances. Spurs keeper George Clawley fumbled a Bert Lipsham shot and pushed the ball out of play. The linesman signalled a corner, but the referee indicated a goal! An entrepreneurial film company was recording the game, and in the following days made a mint from circulating prints of "the goal that never was". But despite the mistake, the goal stood. The majority of the crowd were outraged, and prolonged booing and cat-calling continued until the final whistle.

The replay was in Bolton one week later and there Spurs, watched by 'only' 30,000, secured a 3-1 victory to become the first, and still remain the only, non-League team to win the FA Cup.

Spurs:
Clawley; Erentz, Tait; Morris, Hughes, Jones; Smith, Cameron, Brown, Copeland, Kirwan.

Scorers:
Brown (2)

Attendance:
114,815

Spurs 5 Atletico Madrid 1

European Cup-Winners Cup final, Feyenoord Stadium, Rotterdam, 15th May 1963

Bill Nicholson's great Double side gave its final, and possibly finest, performance on an emotional night in the Dutch port, putting on an exhibition of brilliant football that swept the highly-fancied holders aside.

The Spaniards began with some thundering tackles and Spurs were left in no doubt that their short-passing game would need to be at its best if they were to survive without injury, let alone win the match. A move of stunning speed and simplicity provided the breakthrough after 15 minutes. Bobby Smith, dropping deep, sent Cliff Jones off down the right wing. Jones's inch–perfect cross was met by Jimmy

Jimmy Greaves finds the net as Spurs outclass the Spaniards

Greaves on the half-volley and Spurs had the lead. In the 32nd minute it was Greaves who provided the cross for Smith to dummy. Terry Dyson picked the ball up and slipped it back to John White on the edge of the area. White brought the ball down and unleashed a left footed shot into the net.

Spurs were cruising but, as the second half began, Atletico launched a fierce assault. After just 50 seconds Ron Henry handled on the goal line and Enrique Collar converted the penalty. As the pressure built the Spaniards went close several times, but Danny Blanchflower coolly organised his defensive unit, with Maurice Norman making a colossal effort. A moment of magic from Dyson turned the game. Collecting the ball he flicked it over Feliciano Rivilla and lobbed a curving ball into the centre of the Spanish area. It dipped just under the bar to put Spurs 3-1 up.

Atletico were rocking. On 80 minutes Greaves volleyed in another Dyson cross and, in the final moments, that man Dyson capped the finest display of his career with the goal of the night (see page 42), advancing 40 yards to hammer home from distance as the demoralised defence retreated before him.

Spurs had won, even without the iconic Dave Mackay, and became the first British side to lift a European trophy.

The souvenir programme

Spurs: Brown; Baker, Henry; Blanchflower, Norman, Marchi; Jones, White, Smith, Greaves, Dyson.

Scorers: Greaves (2), White, Dyson (2)

Attendance: 40,000

SPURS 3 MANCHESTER CITY 2

FA Cup final replay, Wembley Stadium, 14th May 1981

The first ever replay of a cup final at Wembley was as memorable as the original game had been anti-climactic.

The quality of the football alone would've made this game special, but it will live long in the memory because of one of the great romantic tales of trial and redemption embodied in the imposing figure of Ricky Villa.

The club issued a commemorative brochure to mark the game

The image of a disconsolate Villa trudging off the pitch after being substituted in the first game was still fresh, but after only eight minutes the big man rifled a shot home from close range after Joe Corrigan parried a fierce strike from Steve Archibald. Three minutes later Tommy Hutchison headed a free-kick down for Steve MacKenzie to volley past Milija Aleksic from 20 yards. It was a beauty and, in most games, that goal would have been the cream of the crop. But this was not most games. Play continued at a frantic pace and a minute later Glenn Hoddle curled a free-kick around a wall of blue shirts, only to strike the post.

Spurs were matching City's work-rate and gradually making their superior skill count, with

only Corrigan denying them. But five minutes into the second half, City were ahead. Dave Bennett went down in the box under challenge from Chris Hughton and Paul Miller, and Kevin Reeves fired the penalty home. Spurs were up against it but, on 70 minutes Hoddle chipped a clearance back into the City box. Archibald controlled it and was about to shoot when Garth Crooks poked the ball into the net.

Seven minutes later Tony Galvin burst down the wing, checked, and rolled the ball to Villa. What followed has been shown on TV many, many times and is described in full on page 50. Ricky Villa's dance through the City defence to score the winner provided a fitting finale to an amazing tale and a thrilling match. Villa's joy was matched by the tens of thousands of Tottenham fans dominating the stadium, and Spurs had triumphed again in a year ending in one. And this time, fittingly, it was the Year of the Cockerel too.

The teams take the pitch for the Centenary Cup Final replay

Spurs:
Aleksic; Hughton, Miller, Perryman, Roberts; Villa, Ardiles, Hoddle, Galvin; Archibald, Crooks.
Scorers:
Villa (2), Crooks

Attendance:
96,000

SPURS 2 CHELSEA 1

League Cup final, Wembley Stadium, 24th February 2008

Despite securing a place in the final courtesy of a spectacular 6-2 aggregate trouncing of Arsenal, Spurs started as underdogs. Chelsea at full-strength were formidable opponents for most teams, and seemed to have a jinx over Spurs.

Spurs put a flag on every fan's seat for the first final at the new Wembley

From the off, Spurs took the game to Chelsea, Robbie Keane going close after Juliano Belletti gifted him the ball in the first minute. Pascal Chimbonda hit the bar from an Aaron Lennon cross, and minutes later Dimitar Berbatov contrived to head wide from six yards. Spurs were on top, Chelsea unable to find their rhythm. Steed Malbranque forced a diving save from Petr Cech with a snapshot from the edge of the area in the 27th minute, but 10 minutes later the tide was turned.

Didier Zokora brought down Didier Drogba on the edge of the box. Spurs goalkeeper Paul Robinson positioned his wall, but then could only watch as

Drogba's kick hit the net. Spurs hit straight back, Keane shooting straight at Cech from a Berbatov flick.

In the second half Lennon switched to the left to torment Belleti but, despite keeping up the pressure, Spurs couldn't find a way through. Then, in the 70th minute, Jermaine Jenas bustled Michael Essien off the ball and released Lennon. The winger's deep cross struck the hand of Wayne Bridge and Berbatov, ice-cool, put the penalty away.

Chelsea, in the words of one report, were "like a punch-drunk boxer hanging on for the final rounds". Keane put Zokora clean through in the 80th minute but the Ivorian's first shot struck Cech in the face, the second was blasted high and wide. Four minutes later Cech pulled off a stunning save to deny Berbatov.

The game went to extra time. After four minutes, Nicolas Anelka, marooned wide on the left, fouled Lennon. Jonathan Woodgate rose to head Jenas's free kick, the ball struck Cech's gloves, rebounded onto Woodgate and pinged back into the net. Chelsea pushed forward but Spurs, now with five in defence, hung on, with Robinson saving from Salomon Kalou in the dying stages.

Programme: £6

Ticket: £65

Winning: Priceless

Spurs: Robinson; Hutton, King, Woodgate, Chimbonda; Lennon, Zokora, Jenas, Malbranque; Keane, Berbatov

Scorers: Berbatov (pen), Woodgate

Attendance: 87,660

SPURS COMIC STRIP HISTORY

4

AFTER AN FA INVESTIGATION INTO FINANCIAL IRREGULARITIES IN 1994, SPURS WERE FINED, DOCKED AN UNPRECEDENTED 12 POINTS, AND BANNED FROM THE FA CUP. CHAIRMAN ALAN SUGAR WAS FURIOUS...

*@$!!

THAT SUMMER ALAN SUGAR INVITED GERMAN SUPERSTAR JURGEN KLINSMANN ON TO HIS LUXURY YACHT...

I WANT TO SEE YOU PLAYING FOR US...

FOR SURE I WILL JOIN THE CLUB...

THE ENGLISH PRESS WENT NUTS!

DON'T BRING FOREIGN CHEATS

SPURS SIGN 'DIVER' KLINSMANN

JURGEN WON THE DAY WHEN HE CELEBRATED SCORING ON HIS DEBUT BY LAUNCHING INTO A SPECTACULAR DIVE BEFORE THE TRAVELLING FAITHFUL!

IF YOU KNOW YOUR HISTORY
MARCHING ON
1977-2010

Relegation reignited the passion among players and supporters and the 1977/78 season saw Spurs play some stunning football in front of huge crowds. Even so, a late wobble meant Spurs only made sure of promotion on goal difference on the last day of the season. But Spurs were back, achieving the feat in proper Spurs style.

The sensational summer signings of World Cup stars Ossie Ardiles and Ricky Villa catapulted the club back into the world spotlight and their abilities, allied to Burkinshaw's hunger for success, the inspired captaincy of Perryman and the sublime skills of Glenn Hoddle, formed the basis of a second glory age. Spurs finished mid-table after a difficult season of adjustment, but the addition of strikers Steve Archibald and Garth Crooks gave them the cutting edge they needed and, in 1981, they reached the Centenary FA Cup final. The full story of that great match is told on page 140, but the win, and a top five hit single, brought back the success and the glamour that had long been missing.

The following season Spurs, now with Ray Clemence in goal, pursued trophies on four fronts, but the sheer number of games got the better of them. They lost a League Cup final to Liverpool, the first Wembley defeat, were kicked out of the UEFA Cup by Barcelona at the semi-final stage and finished fourth in the League. They did retain the FA Cup after a replay in a largely forgettable final against QPR.

An injury to Hoddle, Ardiles's departure after the

Falklands War and financial problems caused by the rebuilding of the West Stand disrupted the following season, one which saw ownership of the club move from the hands of the Wale family and into those of a group of young businessmen headed by Irving Scholar.

The following year, Spurs became the first club to float on the Stock Exchange. Burkinshaw was not enamoured with some of the changes being introduced and in 1984, after his team won its second UEFA Cup

Spurs scooped the world when Keith Burkinshaw signed Ricky Villa and Ossie Ardiles from Argentina

Tony Parks saves Anderlecht's first penalty in the shootout for the 1984 UEFA Cup

after a nail-biting penalty shootout against Anderlecht, he resigned. His assistant Peter Shreeve took over, but was replaced after two seasons by David Pleat.

Pleat reshaped the squad and used a mobile five-man midfield behind pacy striker Clive Allen to put Spurs back into contention for trophies. In 1987 his side finished third in the League, with Allen notching an astonishing 49 goals. But in the FA Cup final Spurs

suffered a shock defeat by Coventry City.

Hoddle left for Monaco and Pleat was sacked
following tabloid revelations. Scholar brought in
Terry Venables, fresh from success at Barcelona. In
the summer of 1988, El Tel began to build his own
squad, signing Pauls Gascoigne and Stewart and adding
superstar striker Gary Lineker the following season.
League finishes of sixth and third were secured, but

Paul Gascoigne's stunning free kick against Arsenal at Wembley in 1991

Spurs were £20million in debt. The was even talk of the club going out of business, unless someone could be persuaded to step in. For this, Spurs needed to be in Europe and with league results poor, only the FA Cup could save them.

Famously, it did, Gascoigne inspiring the team to

another trophy as the year ended in 1, although his contribution to the final against Nottingham Forest was short-lived. On the way came an epic victory over Arsenal in the semi-final,. The 2-1 win saw Spurs qualify for Europe and secure their future.

The financial rescue package came from a deal between Venables and businessman Alan Sugar. Venables became chief executive, brought back Shreeve to manage and began to rebuild the team.

But Sugar and Venables were soon to go their seperate ways amid allegations fought out in court. Sugar took charge and brought in club legend Ossie Ardiles as manager.

As a result of the allegations, Spurs began the 1994/95 season with a 12-point deduction and banned from the FA Cup. Sugar fought the club's corner, eventually overturned the ban and signed a clutch of international stars including – sensationally – the world's number one striker Jürgen Klinsmann.

Spurs played some breathtaking football, but Ardiles's ambitious vision didn't come off. A defeat in the League Cup aganst lowly Notts County proved the final act of his tenure. Gerry Francis and then Christian Gross held the post over the next four years

but it would be former Arsenal boss George Graham who would steer Spurs to success again, his side beating Leicester to win the League Cup in 1999.

Graham would make way for a man whose return was viewed with enormous excitement not just because of his status as one of the club's greatest players, but also because of the managerial success he had achieved. Glenn Hoddle seemed the perfect candidate to lead the club into a new era when ENIC bought the club from Alan Sugar in 2000.

It didn't quite work out, although Hoddle did take his team to another League Cup final in 2002, only to lose to Blackburn in Cardiff.

The club continued to try and lay the foundations for a stable and successful future over the next few years and by the 2005/06 season spent six months in the top four. On a nail-biting final day, Spurs just missed out on qualifying for the Champions League for the first time. The next season brought another fifth-place finish and in 2008 an impressive win over a strong Chelsea team brought the League Cup back to White Hart Lane for the fourth time.

In 2009 Spurs were back at Wembley for yet another League Cup final, this time under the leadership of Harry Redknapp. Manchester United ran out winners, but Redknapp was building an exciting team and in 2010 Spurs finally achieved the breakthrough everyone had been striving for.

After a season of exhilarating football, including a 9-1 demolition of Wigan at home in the league, Spurs secured the coveted fourth spot in spectacular style. Arsenal and Chelsea were beaten in consecutive games at White Hart Lane and then Manchester City outplayed on their own turf in what was effectively a play-off for fourth spot. Spurs were back at Europe's top table and a new chapter awaits.

Ledley King and Robbie Keane celebrate League Cup final victory over Chelsea in 2008

BLUE & WHITE ARMY!

The size and loyalty of Tottenham Hotspur's support has sustained the club through fallow periods on the pitch and provided significant impetus for the club's growth.

In the early years the Spurs crowd, observed *The Football News*, "were not always considerate of the feelings of visiting teams," and it was the need to control rowdy behaviour, as well as the chance to establish a financial base, that prompted the club to charge admission in 1888.

Spurs were rapidly establishing themselves as the team of England's suburban south in an era of dominance by clubs from northern industrial centres. In 1893 the perceived injustice of a FA punishment for practicing "professionalism" gathered further support.

In 1900 Spurs had to win the final game of the season against New Brompton to secure the Southern League title and thousands of Spurs fans swamped the Kent town to see their team lift the trophy. A bigger crowd still turned out to welcome the heroes back to Tottenham, scenes which are said to have inspired Spurs to secure glory on a larger scale in the following season's FA Cup. Famously, they did, with Spurs fans the overwhelming majority in what was then the biggest ever football crowd

Fans leave Euston station in 1937, bound for an FA Cup tie in Cheshire

of 114,000 at Crystal Palace for the final.

A combination of southern pride and a reputation for attractive football kept the crowds coming, with attendances of 40,000 not uncommon even in the lean years of the 1930s. The first Spurs Supporters Club was formed in 1932, not associated with the club but with the aim of organising travel to games. Financial difficulties forced its closure a year later and several other supporter bodies had limited success until 1948, when a second Spurs Supporters Club was established. It published *The Lilywhite* magazine and organised travel and events to which players would regularly come and mix with fans.

Tottenham's glory years in the sixties coincided with a time of optimism after years of austerity and the thrilling football caught the imagination. The Spurs support was not only massive, it was organised and innovative. In 1961 Spurs fans Aubrey Morris and Sid Silver arranged

the first air trip to a game, an FA Cup tie against Sunderland. The business was to grow as Spurs blazed a trail in Europe, culminating in the airlift of 2,500 to Rotterdam for the Cup-Winners' Cup final in 1963. At least 1,500 travelled by car and ferry, at the time the largest ever movement of fans for a game abroad. Morris and Silver's company went on to pioneer the package holiday industry, Morris becoming a director of Thomson Holidays.

Fans cheer their heroes after the 1962 FA Cup win

At around this time Spurs fans were also active in campaigning for greater ticket allocations for fans of the teams who reached cup finals, organising a midnight march from Tottenham to Lancaster Gate.

By now, the noise of the 'Tottenham Roar' was acknowledged by press and players as providing a "twelfth man" at home, especially on European nights and it was the first such night which gave rise to club anthem *Glory Glory Hallelujah*. Opponents Gornik Zabrze had been enraged by Dave Mackay's tough tackling in the first leg, the Polish coach observing Spurs "were no angels". For the return, several Spurs fans dressed as angels and paraded the touchline carrying banners with 'Glory Glory Hallelujah' written upon them.

In 1963, the Tottenham angels appeared on the Cup Winners' Cup victory parade bearing the slogans 'Praise them for they are glorious' and 'Hallowed be thy names'. It was a bit of fun, but it enraged the local vicar, who threatened to report the "blasphemous display" to the Home Office. The fans apologised and the angels were no more. But the anthem lives on.

Relegation in 1977 saw fans rally to cheer the team back into the top flight – adversity as ever drawing fans closer to the club.

The 1980s saw the growth of the football fanzine and supporters' groups which provided fans with a voice independent of the club. As was the case at a number of clubs, some of the fans who began writing for fanzines such as *The Spur*, *Off the Shelf* and *My Eyes Have Seen The Glory* went on to write for the mainstream media. And those original independent groups coalesced into the Supporters Trust, which works alongside the club while retaining an independence of outlook.

The Spurs crowd is opinionated, demanding, always expecting the tradition of flowing football is adhered to and, despite the recent relative lack of success, loyal in number. The 'Tottenham Roar' may be a little quieter in these days of lower capacity all-seater stadiums but the atmosphere generated at White Hart Lane is still capable of sending a shiver down the spine.

This fan looks familiar…

HONOURS AND RECORDS

MAJOR HONOURS
WINNERS
Football League 1951, 1961

Football League Division Two 1920, 1950

FA Cup 1901, 1921, 1961, 1962, 1967, 1981, 1982, 1991

Football League Cup 1971, 1973, 1999, 2008

European Cup-Winners' Cup 1963

UEFA Cup 1972, 1984

FA Charity Shield 1921, 1952, 1962, 1963, 1968 (joint), 1982 (joint), 1992 (joint)

RUNNERS-UP
Football League 1922,1952, 1957, 1963

FA Cup 1987

Football League Cup 1982, 2002, 2009

UEFA Cup 1974

MINOR HONOURS

Southern League Champions 1900

Western League Champions 1904

London League Premier Division 1903

Football League South 'C' Division 1940

Football League South Champions 1944, 1945

Anglo-Italian League Cup 1972

Southern District Charity Cup 1902, 1905 (joint), 1907

London Challenge Cup 1911, 1929

Dewar Shield 1902, 1934, 1935

Norwich Charity Cup 1920

Norwich Hospital Charity Cup 1947, 1950 (joint)

Ipswich Hospital Charity Cup 1952 (joint)

Costa Del Sol Tournament 1965, 1966

Nolia Cup (Sweden) 1977

Japan Cup 1979

Sun International Challenge Trophy (Swaziland) 1983

Peace Cup (Korea) 2005

Vodacom Challenge Trophy (South Africa) 2007

Jubileum Toernooi (Holland) 2008

RECORDS
CLUB

- Most points in a league season: 77, Division One, 1984/85 (3pts for a win); 70, Division Two, 1919/20 (2pts for a win).
- **Most league wins in a season: 31 out of 42 games in 1960/61**
- Most consecutive league wins: 13, 23rd April 1960-1st October 1960
- **Most consecutive home league wins: 14, 24th January 1987-3rd October 1987**
- Most consecutive away league wins: 10, 15th April 1960-29th October 1960
- **Most league goals in a season 115, Division One, 1960/61**
- Record win: Spurs 13 Crewe Alexandra 2, FA Cup 4th Rnd Replay, 3rd February 1960
- **Record league win: Spurs 9 Bristol Rovers 0, Football League Division Two, 22nd October 1977**
- Record defeat: Liverpool 7 Spurs 0, Division 1, 2nd September 1978
- **Record FA Cup win: Spurs 13 Crewe Alexandra 2, FA Cup 4th Rnd Replay, 3rd February 1960**
- Record League Cup win: Spurs 7 Doncaster Rovers 2, 3rd December 1975
- **Record European win: Spurs 9 Keflavik 0, 28th September 1971**

- Highest home attendance: 75,038 v Sunderland, FA Cup 6th Round, 5th March 1938

INDIVIDUAL
- Most appearances (total): Steve Perryman (below), 1014, 1969-1986

- **Most appearances (league): Steve Perryman, 654, 1969-1986**
- Most goals (total): Jimmy Greaves, 266, 1961-70
- **Most goals (league): Jimmy Greaves, 220, 1961-70**
- Most European goals: Martin Chivers, 22 goals in 32 games, 1968-76
- **Most goals in a season (total): Clive Allen, 49, 1986/87**
- Oldest player: Jimmy Cantrell, 39 years, 350 days, v Birmingham City, 21st April 1923
- **Youngest player: John Bostock, 16 years, 295 days, v Dinamo Zagreb, 6th November 2008**
- Consecutive appearances: 247, Ted Ditchburn, 1946-1954
- **Most expensive signing: Darren Bent, £15m (rising to £16.5m) from Charlton Athletic**

FIRSTS AND MISCELLANEOUS RECORDS
- In the Double season of 1961/62,

Spurs won 31 of the 42 league games played. This remains a record for the club, and for the top flight of English football.

- **The first 11 games of that same season were also victories, a record for a winning run in the top flight from the opening match which stands to this day.**
- Spurs were the first team to win the modern Double of top-flight title and FA Cup in the same season.
- **In 1901, Spurs became the first non-League side to win the FA Cup. This record still stands, and is unlikely ever to be broken.**
- That victory also saw Spurs become the first team from the South of England and the first from London to win the FA Cup.
- **In 1963, Spurs became the first British team to win a European trophy, beating Atletico Madrid 5-1 for the Cup-Winners' Cup.**
- When the UEFA Cup was first staged in 1971/72, replacing the old Inter Cities Fairs Cup, Spurs became the first winners, beating Wolverhampton Wanderers over two legs.
- **Spurs hold the British record for consecutive victories in European competition, winning eight times on the bounce**

between 14th September 2006 and 14th March 2007 in that season's UEFA Cup.
- The club remain the most prolific goalscorers of any English club in European competition, scoring an average of 2.1 goals a game.
- **The 2007/08 win over Chelsea made Spurs the first club to win the League Cup at the new Wembley Stadium.**
- Defender Ledley King holds the record for fastest ever Premier League goal, netting after 9.7 seconds against Bradford City in 2000.
- **At 88 metres (96 yards), Paul Robinson's strike for Spurs against Watford on 7th March 2007 is both the longest-range goal scored in Premier League history and the longest-range direct free kick.**
- The 11 minutes and 2 seconds added on to the Stoke City v Tottenham Hotspur game on 19th October 2008 is the longest period of added time ever awarded in the Premier League.
- **Clive Allen holds the record for scoring the most goals in a single League Cup campaign, notching 12 in the 1986/87 season.**